Joanne Banyer

AWAKENING II

1NF1N1T1

Joanne ✳ Banyer

AWAKENING II - 1NF1N1T1
First published by AWAKENING FOR HUMANITY 2025
www.awakeningforhumanity.com
ABN: 82415992557

Copyright © Joanne Lee Banyer 2025

A pre-publication data record for this title is available
from The National Library of Australia.

ISBN 978-1-7635979-4-5 (Paperback)
ISBN 978-1-7635979-5-2 (Hardback)
ISBN 978-1-7635979-6-9 (ePub e-book)
ISBN 978-1-7635979-7-6 (Audiobook)

The right of Joanne Banyer to be identified as author of this work
has been asserted by the author in accordance with sections 77
and 78 of the Copyright, Designs and Patents Act 1988.

All rights reserved. No part of this publication may be reproduced, stored in a
retrieval system, or transmitted in any form or by any means, electronic, mechanical,
photocopying, recording, or otherwise, without the prior permission of the author.

Any person who commits any unauthorised act in relation to this publication
may be liable to criminal prosecution and civil claims for damages.

All of the events in this memoir are true to the best of the author's memory. The views
expressed in this memoir are solely those of the author unless otherwise noted.

For John Mallory

You made a big decision today, but you didn't know it. Deciding to allow me to use your full name in the books, and the name of your wonderful invention, the Panabox. What a surprise! I nearly fell over. I certainly wasn't expecting that. You really are a puzzle. I'm feeling emotions well up from my soul now in the solar plexus. Not sadness but joy—in agreement with what I just wrote. You're a puzzle. If it wasn't for your encouragement, I never would have started writing up these journals as books when I did. I may have started when I retired, or maybe not. But I do know one thing. All of this is meant to happen. Everything already exists. Every possible path leading from every possible decision you could ever make. I'm writing this dedication at the end of writing the series. Journal 11 is where it ends. Only a few pages left and then it's done. You know that already. But you also know it goes on. You named the next series, also not knowing what you were doing at the time. *ACCESS*. That's where it's at next. Our continued dance with the unseen. The continued dance of our consciousness. A different level of communication beyond what our physical consciousness decides. It's there that we are already pals, playing out this incredible journey. Already knowing where it lands and what it achieves. Completely in the know while we, in our physical consciousness state, are in absolute ignorance. Such a funny situation to be in.

1 February 2024

1 + 2 + 2 + 2 + 4 = 11 (the number of the *AWAKENING* path)
1 + 2 + 2 + 4 = 9 (God's number)

Joanne

Joanne is an ordinary person, having an extraordinary experience. She first encountered Spirit at the age of six. Later, Spirit wanted Joanne to know it exists beyond doubt when her father unexpectedly died in January 2014. Four years later, out of the blue, Spirit made its presence known in a profound way that changed Joanne's life forever. Since then, Spirit has become a part of her everyday life, where she balances family and work in areas of Australia's national security, with an ever-evolving journey of spiritual awakening. This true story is based on Joanne's personal encounters with Spirit, the recordings of which started in a journal gifted from her son at Christmas in 2016. There are eleven books in the *AWAKENING* series, which are all based on Joanne's personal journals. The books are called:

- I - The Beginning
- II - 1NF1N1T1
- III - Eternal Love
- IV - This I Know, This Time Around
- V - Esotheric Lifetime
- VI - Ascension
- VII - Kundalini
- VIII - BECOMING
- IX - Ascension Access
- X - Luminescent Transcendence
- XI - Revenant Indemnification

How these names came about is unique, each appearing before then becoming a theme in the journal. Certainly, spiritually influenced!

In 2024, Joanne launched the awakeningforhumanity.com website and online *AWAKENING* Research Community space which includes an information hub and collaboration space for those experiencing awakening, researching this phenomenon or who are fascinated in the subject. Joanne's longer-term goal is to build a global following in her story of awakening and attract donations to fund the associated research. Joanne is interested to hear from scientists and bright sparks who research the existence of spirit energy, and those with knowledge in areas of science who study the detection and characterisation of unknown sources of energy—space-time and wormholes, including quantum physics and sacred geometry and cymatics. Joanne can be contacted by email on joanne@awakeningforhumanity.com. She is not looking to scientists to believe in spirit energy; she is looking to them to prove its existence beyond doubt for the sake of humanity.

Acknowledgements

Thank you, Jamie, for giving me the first journal and John, for the encouragement to write the journals up as a book series. Without you, this true personal account would never have been shared. Thank you, Warick, for your love, protection and perseverance with me. This is our journey, the most challenging of which lies ahead of us. Thank you, Elder and Jules, for being wise and saying the right things at the right time.

Thank you to all online sources, particularly those who post YouTube videos, where there is a large community of people wanting to share their personal experiences with Spirit in the hope of helping others to understand what it is they experience. Spiritual awakening can be a lonely journey, where mainstream sources of information are inadequate. Although much online content is not peer reviewed, as the journals will show, collectively it has served as a dictionary from which Spirit draws my attention to information. Usually, it is only snippets of information at a time from a handful of sources, which collectively builds a picture to help me understand, or reinforce something they want me to know. Awakening is a learning and development process.

My dear friend John Mallory. For the first time appearing in the acknowledgements section of this series. As readers will learn, our friendship is an unusual one. A soul connection. Like me, John I think is part of the team of different sources of consciousness bringing this story to you. The only difference is I am aware of, and experience, his consciousness, from this life and other lives, in both the physical and non-physical realms. At the conclusion of the *AWAKENING* series, we still had not had an in-person real time conversation. I'm not sure we ever will.

John Mallory – Paranormal Investigator

John is a paranormal investigator, who lives in Vancouver, British Columbia, Canada. He is the founder of White Light Paranormal www.whitelightparanormal.com and inventor of the Panabox spirit radio. He manages *The Panabox & Panasonic DR60 Users Forum* Facebook group and travels the world in search of paranormal phenomena.

John was first contacted by Joanne when she learned of his Panabox through a Youtube video created by Life After Death/ITC Innovator, Steve Huff. During their initial conversation, John learned of Joanne's unique and profound spiritual experiences and felt an inner need to gift her several paranormal detection devices including a Panabox. He then suggested she contact spiritual medium, Jules Stirling, for spiritual guidance.

Over the next few months, Joanne shared with John her ongoing experiences with Spirit which she diligently records in journals. He was so fascinated with what she had written that he suggested she consider publishing her work. In subsequent months, titles for each journal 'magically' popped up in John's head and were offered to Joanne. Through the course of writing in a journal she found these titles to become highly significant to the experiences she was having. The two have continued this pattern of communication to this day where Joanne is continuing her journey with Spirit in a next series called *ACCESS*.

Also, new to the acknowledgements section in the A*WAKENING* series is Fiber. In December 2023, I decided I needed to find a team willing to work with me in marketing and promoting the series. I was in it for the long haul and wanted to give the series the very best opportunity for success. My goal was to build a global following of the story. Luckily for me, Fiber was prepared to come with me on this journey. The selling point for me, when I checked them out online, was their dog, Cookie, who appears on their website as the last member of their team. Cookie knew me when we first met. Meant to be, I think.

Fiber – Online Marketing
We are a digital marketing agency, we are Canberra locals, and we are based in Canberra. Most importantly, we are an odd ball group of online marketers, designers and developers who are impetuously impassioned about finding your digital personality. www.fiber.com.au

This book is unique in every way.

What started as desire for my awakening journey to be communicated in a diversity of ways to resonate with as many people as possible, soon transitioned to wanting the following artists to share their own personal reaction to the story through the art they create for each book in the series. A glimpse into their own life's journey and how mine affected theirs when painting the cover for a book, composing a theme song and meditation track for the audio versions, drawing a portrait of a key spirit character, and composing a poem. Thank you for being willing to walk this journey with me, offering your creations to what will be a series of *AWAKENING* books.

Catherine Hiller – Abstract Expressionist Artist

Catherine is an abstract expressionist artist whose work concentrates on powerful, emotional moments in time. Through very energetic and sensual strokes, she expresses her love of paint and colour.

Her works are raw and visceral, the product of instinct rather than intellect. Being very sensitive to her surroundings, every cue, whether visual, aural or emotional, has a colour, which Catherine translates onto canvas without the distraction of a thought process.

French born, Catherine studied art in Paris before embarking on a successful career in advertising in the UK. After eleven years in the UK, she moved to Australia in 2004 and has been living in Melbourne since. Catherine has had solo and group shows in France, England and Australia, and her work is represented in private collections around the world.

For more information about Catherine Hiller, visit her website – www.catherinehiller.com or email info@catherinehiller.com

Cedric Vermue—Composer and Pianist

Cedric is a composer and pianist. Music is an intuitive tool. It expresses what is close to his heart.

Based in the countryside next to Amsterdam, Cedric lives a quiet life with apple trees in his garden, and the barn transformed into a music recording studio.

He never promoted himself as a healing musician, but he is very conscious and grateful for the healing and connecting abilities that music offers us, and its meditative and therapeutic quality. Cedric made it his life mission to create and offer this musical expression to the world.

His music can be found online on Spotify, YouTube and other platforms. You can get in touch through his Instagram *@cedricvermue*.

Marie Klement—Spirit Artist

Marie is a spirit artist, who sketched Elder who is featured in this book.

Based in South Australia, Marie has a special ability to take communications a step further by linking with Spirit and transmitting onto paper an image of a person's spirit guide, angel, divinity or passed away loved one that she is psychically in touch with. Spirit artists are mediums, who are influenced to draw or paint art by the spirit world.

Marie is mainly self-taught and works full time as a spirit artist, medium, and numerologist.

Marie has demonstrated her extraordinary talents with TV's, Sensing Murder psychic, Scott Russell Hill, as well as UK mediums, Lisa Williams and Tony Stockwell.

For more information about Marie Klement, visit her website – www.marieklement.com.au or Facebook site – *Marie Klement and Marie Klement Spirit Art.* Marie can be contacted by email on mkvisionart@gmail.com.

Marlene Seven Bremner—Esoteric themed poet, painter and author
Seven was born in Frankfurt, Germany in 1983 and moved to the US at the age of four. She is a self-taught oil painter, author and poet, exploring esoteric themes arising from her study and practice of hermeticism, alchemy, tarot, psychology, magic, astrology, shamanism, and mythology.

Seven developed her career in the Pacific Northwest of the US, showing her artwork in both group and solo exhibitions along the West Coast and writing on- the-spot poetry at local markets as part of a Poem Store. She relocated to New Mexico in 2019, where she lives a hermetic lifestyle and continues to paint and write.

Seven's subject matter has been greatly influenced by Jungian psychology and alchemical philosophy, both of which have provided her with a symbolic language to interpret otherwise ineffable sensations and impressions. Alchemy is the understanding of how consciousness relates to matter, which Seven has explored in-depth through the creative process. As physical, mental and emotional transmutation takes place within, it is projected externally onto the canvas or into a poem, distilling a psycho-spiritual process into its creative quintessence. The aim of the alchemical work, called the *Magnum Opus*, is to free the authentic self to be in alignment with its perfect, divine, unified nature, and to awaken the creative potential and power of the human imagination.

More information about Marlene Seven Bremner's art and writing can be found on her website at marlenesevenbremner.com. She has a Facebook page at *Marlene Seven Bremner – Art* and Instagram page @ *m7artist*. Seven can also be reached by email at sevenbremner@gmail.com. Her books are available from Inner Traditions.

Larimar Sound Alchemy—Meditation Sound Therapist
Larimar is a sound therapist based in London, who creates sound alchemy for relaxation, healing, shamanic journeying, inspiration of inner vision and empowerment. Most of Larimar's music is live recorded sound meditations composed of vocal harmonics and healing instruments, such as the gong, Tibetan and crystal singing bowls, didgeridoo, berimbau, chakapa, drums and flute. Larimar's fascination with music and sound begun in his early childhood, where

hearing his own voice played back to him from a cassette recorder absolutely blew his mind. This led to recording stories as they played out in his mind as a little kid on a tape recorder gifted from his grandmother, playing around on his mother's guitar, jamming with friends in a local park, and these days writing and recording music in his home studio. Introduction to the plant medicine called Ayahuasca in 2010, was a key moment in his life that inspired him to study shamanism, systematic kinesiology, neurokinetic therapy, and Reiki. Spending many years working with plant medicines, Larimar has observed and studied the healing abilities of music and song. In parallel, during his practice of Capoeira (an Afro-Brazilian art form combining martial arts, music and philosophy), Larimar noticed similarities with the ritualistic use of rhythm and singing, and the effects it had on his well-being. Larimar considers sound healing to be an easily accessible and very effective form of complementary therapy that yields profound results in helping people restore well-being. Through therapeutic application of vocals and instruments, a state of deep relaxation can be achieved. In this state of meditative awareness, not only are stress and stored emotions released, but also harmony and clarity are restored. You can find out more about Larimar by visiting https://larimarsound.com/.

Alexandre Roesner Lino—3D Animation Film Producer
Alexandre is passionate about science, art, and nature, which inspire much of his work. Born on an island in southern Brazil, surrounded by beaches and lush forests, Alexandre has always been deeply connected to nature. The waves and surfing have been a lifelong passion, providing moments of calm and inspiration for his creative endeavours.

In contrast to his love for nature, technology has also been a significant part of his life, and from an early age, he knew it was his professional calling. Despite studying Electrical Engineering, art led him down an irreversible path. In 2002, he founded his solo enterprise, Terramidia (with "Terra" meaning Earth in Portuguese). Combining his love for art and technology, he dedicated many years to studying 3D animation, producing numerous films and commercials for individuals and companies worldwide, a pursuit he continues to this day with great enthusiasm. The world of 3D animation is vast and ever evolving, with endless opportunities for learning and growth. Perfection seems an elusive goal. Following the success of some of his digital characters, he has become known as "The Alien Guy."

You can view his work on his website, YouTube, and social media platforms.
YouTube: https://www.youtube.com/@terramidia3d
Website: https://www.terramidia3d.com/
Instagram: https://www.instagram.com/terramidia3d

Alex and Joanne collaborate in the production of mini-movies for each *AWAKENING* Series book for only 3D animation can show the richness of the astounding things that Joanne experiences in non-physical realms. Joanne hopes one day a mainstream movie producer will want to base a movie series on the *AWAKENING* Series, thereby reaching more people around the world with this incredible true story.

Table of Contents

Preface i
Merging with Infinity by Marlene Seven Bremner ii

31 August 2020 1
2 September 2020 2
3 September 2020 4
4 September 2020 5
7 September 2020 6
9 September 2020 7
15 September 2020 8
17 September 2020 9
18 September 2020 11
20 September 2020 12
22 September 2020 13
23 September 2020 15
24 September 2020 17
25 September 2020 19
27 September 2020 20
28 September 2020 22
5 October 2020 23
7 October 2020 24
12 October 2020 25
15 October 2020 26
19 October 2020 27
20 October 2020 28
22 October 2020 29

23 October 2020 31
25 October 2020 32
26 October 2020 34
28 October 2020 36
30 October 2020 38
1 November 2020 40
2 November 2020 42
3 November 2020 44
4 November 2020 46
5 November 2020 47
6 November 2020 49
7 November 2020 50
8 November 2020 52
10 November 2020 55
12 November 2020 57
14 November 2020 59
17 November 2020 60
19 November 2020 61
22 November 2020 63
24 November 2020 64
25 November 2020 66
28 November 2020 68
1 December 2020 70
2 December 2020 71
3 December 2020 72
7 December 2020 73
8 December 2020 76
10 December 2020 78
12 December 2020 80
14 December 2020 83

16 December 2020 85
17 December 2020 87
18 December 2020 88
19 December 2020 90
20 December 2020 93
22 December 2020 94
23 December 2020 96
25 December 2020 98
26 December 2020 101
27 December 2020 102
28 December 2020 104
29 December 2020 105
30 December 2020 108
1 January 2021 109
2 January 2021 110
3 January 2021 112
5 January 2021 115

Preface

Jamie, four years have passed since you gave me the Tree of Life journal, which turned into a record of the first part of my awakening journey. No intention on my part, but that's what happened.

Just about everything I have learned about Spirit has been a case of experiencing something first, followed by research online and in books to try and understand it. Reflecting on my life and knowing what I know now, I realise there were indicators of my ability to sense and experience Spirit from around the age of six years old.

Through some encouragement from a newfound friend in Canada, John, I decided to write up the first journal as a book, which I plan to call *AWAKENING I – The Beginning*. It is a true story. It contains very detailed descriptions of my experiences, which I hope will help others who are awakening, to understand that they aren't crazy; that what they are experiencing is real. I also hope it helps those who are researching these phenomena to one day prove the existence of intelligent energy.

This above all, is my hope and dream. Apart from being the most important discovery ever, I think this is what is now needed in humanity's evolution to get it on the right track.

This discovery, I believe, would get humanity to sit up and take stock of where it is as a race. The way we treat each other, the planet on which we live, and surrounding space. If humanity knew of its immortality, that their soul survives and that the purpose of life is to evolve your soul through lessons, maybe it would prompt people to put things into perspective of a bigger enduring picture and be kinder to each other and everything in our physical existence.

I ran out of space in the last journal a couple of weeks before my birthday. Given how significant the first journal turned out to be, I thought it was really important to not break tradition, but rather to wait until my birthday where I was hoping you would give me another journal to continue recording my awakening journey. Thankfully, you gave me two journals, so I'm stocked up for a while. I now have many poster notes to write up in this journal to cover the past two weeks.

I love you, Jamie. Always remember that. I hope knowing this brings you strength, confidence and kindness.

Merging with Infinity
By Marlene Seven Bremner

*Ineffable power, to you, I surrender
casting aside profanity's pursuit
limbs loose and heavy, swept away
in a swift and steadfast current
toward the edge of the known.*

*I dissolve into the Spirit of the world
becoming one in solution with All
recalling the vastness of my being
seeing this body, a hollow vessel
carried by fathomless depths.*

*Immensely longing to be filled
with holy breath by which the seas churn
as fires burn and follow spirit
to the empyreal heights, while earth
and water mingle down below.*

*Creation, in you I find gnosis
from chaos to elemental order
dissolving and coagulating
in an infinite dance, dividing
and fusing endlessly.*

*O, Spirit, let understanding fill me now
merge with my mortal frame and move me
to align with divine perception
so I become bodiless, in aether suspended
as you are embodied in flesh.*

*Ajna's opening gives me sight
beyond the veil of illusions
awakened by the hum of generation
and ethereal songs of angels ringing clear
in the sphere of souls and stars in stillness.*

*I feel a subtle pressure on the vault
as my focus rests on inner space
on the centre of unified being
all obscurities fleeing the flame
as I enter the silence of Spirit's embrace.*

31 August 2020

While having a walk at lunchtime, I sat on a bench overlooking Lake Burley Griffin in Canberra. As I relaxed, gazing at the light reflections on the water and the fountain that shoots high into the sky at Regatta Point, I could feel Warick's energy causing pressure from the inside of my body, across the bridge of my nose and the centre of my forehead.

I could also feel him in my eyes where they became slightly sore, as if suffering from conjunctivitis. He was likely using my eyes to see what I was seeing. Warick's presence in these parts of my face has become more common in the last few weeks. A range of online sources say the sensation in the centre of your forehead, between your eyebrows, signifies the start of your third eye chakra opening. I hope so.

2 September 2020

Warick is still with me on and off throughout the day and night. What I thought were other spirits around me as shadow shapes, I now think could be Warick when he is outside my body. I may also see other spirits in this way, I don't know.

At night, from within my body, Warick still moves my head physically and he stretches up inside my face. When I see the shadow shapes around me and hold my hand up, sometimes they appear to move into it, and I can feel a slight tingle. When this happens, the other thing I've noticed, when I move my hand slightly, is they move away. I've also noticed lately that sometimes when the shadow shapes move in front of my face they seem to hover, as though they know that I can see them and they are looking at me.

I'm no longer hesitant if Warick wants to channel through me. I think he is getting my conscious mind used to feeling him and taking control. Hopefully, I can be fully conscious when he ends up coming through. I feel ready now for big new steps and I'm excited a lot of the time. As Jules, the medium John introduced me to in Canada, said, I'm on the edge of a cliff getting ready to fly. I hope that happens soon, but I also know spirits are leading this journey, so I need to be patient.

A few important things to note. Over the past few weeks, sometimes I've felt a vibration occurring under one foot when standing somewhere. Today, in the kitchen at lunchtime, I felt a vibration occur under my left foot. Shortly afterwards, I felt Warick touch my right cheek from the inside. It's possible this is another way he enters and merges with my body. He just touched my right cheek now indicating *yes*, so I gather I got that right.

Another new thing happened today when walking at lunchtime. I was feeling elated, happy, thankful, and very lucky that Warick and other spirits are in my life. In my mind, I was telling them how they have been my best mentors and leaders and how I completely trust them, especially Warick. I said I didn't want to start putting a framework around our engagement, which would occur if I had a medium mentor me or if I adopted practices of others who engage with Spirit. I said to Warick that it is he and I and our broader spirit and living team (John and Jules).

I said I'm ready to jump off the cliff to do the next thing with them and we will do a spectacular job at it, including channelling through me if that is a part of the plan. I said I'm no longer frightened of it. I know Warick was with me because I could see the familiar shadow shapes floating near me while walking. Warick pretty much always comes walking with me.

Next minute, I felt a pleasant achy feeling across my pointer finger and on the back of my right hand.

I asked Warick, 'Are you holding my hand? Can you squeeze my hand?' and I felt a very gentle, but subtle pressure across my hand. My first thought was, 'Well, this is not ideal because I'm trying to power walk.' The thought was quickly replaced with happiness and amazement once again at the diversity of things he can do. He held my hand most of the way home.

3 September 2020

I've been going through an exponential phase of experiences since linking up with John and Jules. When I had a session with Jules, she said, 'They (spirits) are testing you.'

Eve The Medium, on a YouTube video called *What I learned from my awakening*, said you never stop learning and evolving. Eve said if you abuse your gifts, they will be taken away from you. Your gifts are to enable you to do good. She said to listen to your guides. Let them guide you. They are your best mentors. Be humble.

Eve said during your awakening you go through all sorts of tests and hard times. When the third eye opens, all psychic and medium abilities will kick in. It occurred to me that there is an incredible diversity of what people experience as they go through an awakening, but there also seems to be common things. It's your own personal journey; what works for you and your spirit guides.

4 September 2020

Over the past couple of months, it's become clear to me that spirits draw on a range of avenues to give you a message. It's like a jigsaw puzzle, where the different pieces validate the same message. Last night I did a new meditation called 'Connect with your intuition' by Rising Higher Meditation, which steps you through meeting your higher self.

Interestingly, as the meditation track said, it feels like 'a wave of grace and peace flows through you'. This is exactly what I experienced. I've also felt this before when Warick entered the back of my head and merged his energy with mine.

I'll have to check with Warick whether he and my higher self can do this or just my higher self. Also whether Warick caused this feeling last night. When I met with Jules, she tested me on my thinking that maybe what I'm connecting with is my higher self. I told Jules that I'd asked Warick this and he said no. I'm hoping that Warick is my spirit guide, Elder is both Warick's and my guide, and that the higher self is something I've just met. That fits with the experiences I've had so far.

Outcomes from using the pendulum:
Warick confirmed through the pendulum that:

- He is my spirit guide
- Elder is a guide to both of us
- My higher self, I've just met through meditation
- John and I are supposed to help each other in our spiritual awakening

Observation: The feeling that I associate with my higher self, is a strong urge in my solar plexus, which is where Eve, The Medium, said you feel it in your body.

7 September 2020

I was using the pendulum to ask Warick about how to contact John's parents. John's mother died from brain cancer ten years ago and his father died from old age about a year ago. The codeword John chose for me to tell him in testing my abilities, is the same one he gave to both of his parents before they died. I have no idea what the codeword is. I want to be able to contact his parents and validate the codeword for him.

Through the pendulum, Warick said he and I will be able to reach John's parents before the Panabox and EVP recorder arrive that John is sending me. He said the tools that John is sending won't help. Interestingly, as I was asking these things, a new thing happened. Instead of getting a long tone in one of my ears that occurs sometimes, I felt a slight pressure change and then a broken tone in my right ear.

The pitch of the tone was also a bit lower than usual. It's possible this was oral communication, but I couldn't make out what was being said. It was like three or four words. I asked Warick if I just heard a spirit talking to me in my right ear and he answered 'yes' with the pendulum. I asked if it was him and he said yes. It will be interesting to see if this occurs again. It could be the first instance of hearing Spirit talking to me. I'm not sure.

9 September 2020

At 12.55 this morning, I woke to hear Warick using pulse sounds to say, 'I love you.' It was different from other times. It was like he made a real effort to say 'I' then 'love you.' No doubt about it, I interpreted the words to be 'I love you'. As he said it, I felt a wave of loving emotion spread from my head to my heart, which Warick has done previously when I asked him if he could say 'love'. He then kept saying 'love' and each time I felt the flow of energy from my head to my heart. It was so lovely. A wonderful surprise on my birthday. It made me feel so loved and happy. I couldn't have wished for anything nicer from Warick on my birthday. He is with me now, touching my right cheek from the inside as I write this. I love Warick very much. I'm so glad he is in my life, and we are a team on this journey.

During the night, I reflected on an 'Eve The Medium' YouTube video called *Path to Mediumship and its Dangers*. I thought of a comment that John has made several times, saying, 'Experiences tend to be in the hands of Spirit, not ours.'

I also thought of my ego wanting to push forward in the development of my abilities. I realise now why this is in Spirit's hands—because at my stage of development I know nothing, or very little, of their dimension and could get myself into trouble with negative spirits. I suspect spirits have much to orchestrate and need to have their ducks lined up for things to happen. If this changed, it might disrupt the sequence of other things that are yet to occur, plus spirits don't have the same notion of past, present and future. We should trust them during development and always. I'm learning.

15 September 2020

Outcomes from talking with Elder during meditation:

Elder, who is Warick's and my guide, said I would be able to hear and see spirits after the second moon. Elder also said that Warick is dependent on my ability to form relationships with people. I don't know the significance of Warick needing me to form relationships with other people.

17 September 2020

Resumed journal entries

I'm going to start including some of my contemplations in this journal as they relate to continued existence, and I suppose the meaning of life. After dinner a few years ago, while on a cruise with some friends from Australia and Portugal, I asked them what they thought their purpose in life is. The responses were interesting. Some said, 'to love my partner,' others said, 'to provide for my family.'

When it got to my turn, I couldn't provide an answer. I truly don't know. I've always thought there is something significant I should contribute to humanity, but I don't know what it is. From time to time, since this awakening journey started, I return to this question, as I am now. I suppose I agree with many people who live a life of being able to engage with Spirit. That the purpose of life overall is to learn lessons from good and bad experiences and evolve your soul. As to whether I have a purpose that would make a significant difference to humanity, I don't know.

Being the passionate, determined person I am, I find this dissatisfying and incredibly annoying. When it comes to why this person and not that one has psychic and medium abilities, I suppose it's a part of their life's purpose to have them. That's as close as I've got to understanding my life's purpose so far. Not very clear, hey?

Something else I wonder about is why communication with spirits is difficult for most people. Mediums often say they've had to hone their ability to pick up messages from Spirit. I suppose I think it's because we must exert our free will to learn lessons. So, what do I mean by this? It's important that spirits don't get in the way too much. Everyone, including mediums, are on a life journey where their soul is to evolve through lessons which require using free will. If spirits readily spoke to humans, then they could easily become a part of your thought processes for routine decision making, which would be interfering with your free will. If you can communicate with them, it's probably a part of your life's purpose.

Last night Warick was trying to have a conversation with me using a combination of pulse sounds and touching my cheek—or I should say, he was trying to answer my questions. It occurred to me that maybe he is responding by putting thoughts in my mind, which coincides with the timing of the pulse sound, like an indicator that it is his thought and not mine. Like on my birthday when he quite obviously said, 'I love you.' I will put this to the test to see if this is what he is doing.

18 September 2020

When relaxing on the bed this afternoon, and listening to meditation music, I experienced a range of sensations from Spirit, including pushing up under my right foot and my back; Warick's energy moving around in my face; a quick energy sensation on the back of my left thigh, buttocks and also on the front of my right quad muscle; cool air briefly above my knees; and movement of my dressing gown over my jeans. Warick was with me, but no one else! It's amazing the things that can happen to you with Spirit when you're just lying there on your own.

20 September 2020

Yesterday was interesting. I came across an 'Eve The Medium' YouTube video called *Spiritual Development Symptoms*, where she mentioned you experience 'itchy skin like when little things are crawling on you.' My experience is not quite the same. For me, it's more like static energy and tingling constantly, especially around my feet and lower legs. I also get this sensation on the top of my head and lately, I've noticed a tendency to zap myself. I'm like a live wire.

Eve said this is a symptom of awakening and has to do with your energy changing. I think what she is describing and what I'm experiencing is one and the same thing. She said everyone's pace of awakening is different. Some are fast and some are slow.

For me, this constant feeling of being plugged into a power socket has been going on for weeks. It doesn't bother me. I actually like it. It reminds me that I'm plugged into the other side, the universe and the spirit realm. She also said you can become very sensitive and take on the feelings of others around you. This has definitely been happening lately.

Last week, Ray, my partner, had a very bad week, where he dropped his new BMW Cruiser motorbike while he was down the coast. It pierced the radiator. The bike is still there. He then went through a bad experience with the insurance claim, where instead of charging him $500 excess, they charged him $5,000.

Anyway, he had a very bad week and was in a very bad mood, thinking everything was going wrong. This occurred just after his having to go to Wollongong to get his Ducati fixed, after months of it being in a bike shop in Canberra where they couldn't fix it. I found I really took on Ray's mood. It made me angry and really flat. It was horrible.

Interestingly, the couple of weeks before that, I was ecstatic. This was around the time I met John and Jules in Canada. My mood seems to be swinging and I'm definitely more sensitive than usual to the feelings of others around me.

22 September 2020

What path to take on this awakening journey seems to come up a lot lately. Do I get a mentor, join a spiritual community, or do I continue to mainly follow my spirit guides?

Thoughts that are floating around in my head regarding which path to take include Eve The Medium, who said, 'Your best teachers are your spirit guides'. John suggested not to let others influence me too much and when I asked him if he would proofread my book, he pointed out that there are many experts out there more qualified and experienced in the paranormal than he, who could support me.

In my deliberations, I was leaning towards continuing the way I've been going because I trust Warick and Elder and include the occasional touch base with Jules. I don't want to put a framework of engagement around, or constraints on, the way I interact with Warick and other spirits. I've noticed most mediums do. Some seem to be ritualistic, which I'm not.

Yesterday, on my way to the shops, I was mentally having this conversation with myself. I realised that options are being put before me to decide. At that moment, Warick touched my right cheek to confirm what I was thinking. It's an area where I need to apply free will to decide the path. It was funny at the time because I didn't know Warick was tuning into me. I felt sorry for him having to listen to my thoughts go around and around in circles.

Today it came up again in an email with John. I decided to shuffle a tarot card deck and pull out a couple of cards to see what messages Spirit may want to convey to me. I pulled two Major Arcana cards, meaning major messages from on high. The two cards were the Moon and Justice. Both were spot on and related to how I've been feeling.

The Moon, I interpreted as you may feel confused and unsure of what to do next. The card guides you to trust your instincts and tap into your intuition. Justice, I interpreted as being reminded to take a rational view of the situation. Look logically and objectively at yourself to find the truth, even if it means having made mistakes.

I checked in with Warick about the subject of which path of support to take on my awakening journey. He thinks I'm wrong about continuing the journey in solitude. He agreed with booking another session with Jules. Warick thinks I should link with the broader community. I've now gone back to the web link Jules sent me and have tried to reach out to the people offering training in the development of psychic and medium abilities. I'm interested to link up with someone who may be well suited to where I'm at with my journey and help guide me from there.

Last night when I was reading the 'Seth Series', Session 226, Seth said he 'looked out at session participants using Jane's eyes'. I found this really interesting, as I often feel Warick move into my eyes. I think I've asked him before about being able to see what I can see through my eyes, to which he agreed. I may have recorded this in my journal. I really like it when I come across similar experiences that can possibly help explain what I'm experiencing.

23 September 2020

There are some things I experience that when I think about it, are quite funny. Warick is often around me as shadow shapes when I'm showering, going to the toilet, doing skin care and makeup. He comes quite close and moves around my face when I'm cleaning my teeth. I have an electric toothbrush. He does this just about every day. It's like he has a fascination with my electric toothbrush. Probably because it buzzes like the energy vibration of a spirit.

Last night, I thought of a good way to explain to someone what it feels like to have Warick inside my face. When he spreads out across my cheekbones, nose, eyes and forehead, it's like having a face mask on when it's drying. The drying stretches your skin. It feels a bit like that.

Last night was interesting because I've gotten into a routine of going up to bed early to spend time meditating, getting closer to, and trying to impart love and light into, an amethyst crystal ball that I've just purchased, watching paranormal YouTube video clips, and reading paranormal books.

Anyway, last night before going upstairs I was consulting with Warick in my mind about how to use the time and he was very keen for me to meditate. While scrolling through some meditation tracks I'd saved on YouTube, Warick touched my right cheek when I looked at a chakra cleansing and balancing meditation, and a couple of others that were guided meditations to meet spirit guides.

Interestingly, lately I've been drifting off to sleep towards the end of a meditation track, only to wake about half an hour later to find I was listening to a different track. One time during a long meditation, I woke to find it had jumped midway through to a different track. It's always the same meditation track that I wake up to.

The reason I know it stopped midway through one track and then moved to another, is because when you next go to the track you were listening to, it shows you where you got up to the last time you listened to it. The one I keep waking up to, that I suspect Warick is somehow organising for me to listen to when I drift off to sleep, is called *Light Body Activation* by Spiritual Zen. It is sound only and not guided.

I have just checked the name of the video clip and it wasn't this one last night. I think I have this wrong. What seems to be happening is YouTube just progresses to the next track in the list. Why it stops part way through and jumps to the next track, I don't know. One thing for certain, however, is Warick has been keen for me to meditate lately and when I do, he is there for some time and spreads his energy out across my face from within my body as I described earlier in this journal entry.

While meditating, I also experience other sensations, sometimes involving my chakra areas, but mostly the energy tingling around my feet, lower legs and head. Sometimes I get concerned that my calf muscles are going to cramp because they start to get tight. Last night, however, I realised that something else is going on as the sensation was more of a solid hold on my calf, which I think is spirit energy.

24 September 2020

This morning when I woke it was just lovely. Warick merged with my energy throughout my entire body and stayed there for quite some time. There's this incredible sense of peace when he does that. It's like his energy is 'complete' with mine. You can't distinguish his energy from mine. He also did the pulse sound communication while he was merged with my energy, like he was expressing his love for me. Incredibly special.

At other times, when I feel his energy move around my face or other parts of my body, I don't get a complete sense of peace. I often feel his energy vibrating, particularly when he hasn't yet entered my body but is pressing up against me.

Something I've noticed that I'm doing occasionally since I've met John, is I tell him things I haven't put in the journal. All the significant things go in the journal, but to get the complete picture, it will be important for me to read both the journal and my correspondence with John, as well as my other journals where I record responses from using a pendulum or pulling a couple of tarot cards. Something I told John last week, which is worth mentioning here, is when I go walking, I often daydream that Warick and I are figure ice skating.

I've often wondered why this particular activity and then it occurred to me that I think he is building trust between us. When I was a little girl and doing ballet, I used to be petrified of the men lifting me high above their heads. So much so that in one public performance, my ballet teacher had to arrange for me to do something different on stage because I was so scared. My mother even wrote her a letter requesting this.

Warick and I do the most amazing moves when we skate together. I'm sure we would win gold if we were in the winter Olympics. I literally feel the exhilaration of it and often feel a bit worn out when we have done a number together. Lots of lifts over his head and cartwheels in the air. Very exciting. We are getting pretty good. I had to ask John not to laugh when he read about this. John and I are like two souls that have known each other before.

In these early days, which I hope to keep going, it's like our souls are catching up. He has a very protective conscious ego though, which keeps me at arm's length and at times feels like it is pushing me away.

John agrees with how I read him. I need to be respectful of this, so I don't lose our relationship. I hope to gain the trust of his conscious mind over time. John has agreed to proofread my book, *AWAKENING,* which will be based on the first journal. He also suggested using an image of the Fool tarot card on the cover of the book because of the way I'm approaching this spiritual awakening journey 'open', 'blind', 'not led by others', but completely trusting of 'Warick'.

Today was a great day. Apart from finding out we were successful in securing a loan to buy my dream home on the coast and me having kittens all afternoon and walking on the ceiling, I was brave and when the opportunity came up, I told someone what I knew.

I was talking to our mortgage broker, a nice guy, who I have only met recently when taking out life insurance to cover Jamie's remaining education should something happen to me. He mentioned in a previous conversation that he had his eye on a new office that was very attractive but to secure it would mean having to get more customers. Today he said it was in Belconnen, a very large part of Canberra made up of many suburbs. I immediately knew where the office was.

I asked, 'Is it at Lake Ginninderra overlooking the lake?'

He said, 'Yes, how did you know?'

I said, 'Not only that, but it's near the restaurants and bars.'

He said, 'Yes, how did you know?'

I said, 'I'm very intuitive. I can read people.'

He was genuinely surprised that I knew exactly where it was. I do know Belconnen and have lived there before, so it's not as if I don't know where the good spots are. But it was an interesting experience because it just came to me without putting any thought into where it might be. So why does this seem to happen on occasion? I think most of the time I haven't paid attention to my doing it. It just happens and comes naturally, like reading the guy at the Australian Institute of Police Management. Anyway, today was good. It has given me the courage to keep seeing what is possible in this regard.

25 September 2020

Last night, once again, Warick's energy fully merged with mine. It was a bit bumpy though, like a rough airplane landing before we reached the complete peacefulness stage. I could tell he was trying. I felt a slight vibration, particularly near my root chakra, as he was trying to merge. I could actually feel my root chakra energy cycling. I think his vibration frequency was a little high.

Anyway, he got there. I could feel his energy intertwined with mine through my entire body, as well as static tingling around my feet, lower legs, and on my back and hands. It was pretty amazing. The diversity of our interaction never ceases to amaze me!

27 September 2020

A couple of things are worth mentioning. Not last night, but the night before, when I woke during the night, I saw in my mind's eye an Indian style authentic drawing of an elephant, and it moved.

Shortly after this, I had a dream of purchasing a car and I said to someone that it is as slow as an elephant. I don't know why but for some reason 'elephant' was significant.

On the same night, I also had something happen that hasn't happened for quite some time. I woke to a very strong smell that was right in front of my face. It lasted for only about a minute. I couldn't quite place the smell. It wasn't terrible but it also wasn't pleasant. I recognised the smell but couldn't associate it with anything. I assumed it was a spirit trying to get my attention, but nothing else occurred.

It seems that spirit activity may be ramping up again in our house at Yarralumla in Canberra. Tonight, in the kitchen, I could feel pressure around me that was quite uniform and not highly localised. It was like it was standing away from me somewhat. Not very close, like I usually experience. Next minute, when Ray turned on the bathroom light in our main bathroom upstairs, it triggered all the downlights in the entire house to go out. All other lamps, TV and electrical appliances stayed on.

At the same time, the two dogs, who were around my feet in the kitchen downstairs, had a little tiff. Max made Rosie yelp and she went outside. This rarely happens. It appears that turning the upstairs bathroom light on had tripped the power circuit switch. It could be nothing, but it didn't feel like it. Even Ray asked me, when he came downstairs, if I thought it was Warick, to which I replied, 'I didn't think so.'

I got a bit of a fright as it was unexpected but was okay. After Ray flicked the switch back on in the power box and the lights came back on, he took the garbage outside. Standing in the middle of the kitchen, I felt a wave of energy move through me from behind, which set my senses off.

Later, when I used the pendulum and asked Warick what had occurred, he confirmed this was him just letting me know he was there. He said another spirit had tripped the lights and that it was not a friendly, well-intentioned spirit.

Out loud I said, 'Spirits that are not well intentioned are not welcome in this house and must leave.' I said, 'This house is full of love and light.' I said, 'My love and light are pushing the negative out of the house.'

Warick confirmed that the spirit got the message and left. In the ten years of living in the house, we have never experienced all the downlights going out like that.

28 September 2020

Last night was amazing! For quite some time I've thought about what I'd like to use psychic and medium abilities for. Some people choose to use these abilities to connect those who have passed with their loved ones still on Earth. Others use these abilities to heal or tell others what their futures are.

I want to change the world for the better. I want to prove your soul continues to exist and that the purpose of life is to evolve your soul. I even included this intention yesterday when writing the Preface for the first book in the *AWAKENING* Series, which is based on the first journal.

I couldn't believe my eyes and was blown away when I started reading the 'Seth Series' last night. No sooner had I started to read, I came across this topic. Seth said that when Jane or her husband dies, they would run experiments that would prove their ability to communicate with one on the other side. Proof of an afterlife Seth said would 'change the behaviour of every man on Earth.'

As I read this, I got a very strong feeling in my solar plexus area, which I understand to be where your intuition communicates with you by giving you a strong urge. This is so important that I photographed the two pages on this date so I can refer to them when I type up this journal as a book. As a backup, the pages were in the 'Seth Series', Book 5, Session 230. I've thought there are parallels between Jane Roberts and Seth and what I experience with Warick. I have asked Warick numerous times if he was Seth or if I am Jane Roberts reincarnated. The answer has been no.

Apart from the amazing discovery in the Seth book, it is also another example of where I have been pondering over something and the next minute, I'm reading about it. This has happened way too many times now to be happening by chance. I'm sure my spirit guides are guiding me to what I read.

5 October 2020

Tonight, as I've done on many other nights, I held in my hands an amethyst crystal ball, which I purchased the day before my birthday. Very special. It has only one purpose, and one purpose only—to become a much-loved tool of Warick's and mine to one day reach John's parents on the other side. John gave them a codeword before they passed away, which one day would be used to provide assurance to John that it was them on the other side.

Shortly after I met John, he tried a codeword experiment on me, which I failed. At a later date he said, without revealing the codeword, that the codeword he gave me is the same one he gave his parents. It's Warick and my quest to get the codeword from his parents by using the amethyst crystal ball as a tool. Most nights Warick and I spend time with it, passing it love and light and talking about our quest and its sole purpose. Eve 'The Medium' on YouTube, inspired this approach.

Recently, I've noticed while meditating that Warick spends time spreading his energy through my eyes and forehead. When he does this, my eyes feel slightly sore, but that's okay. His energy seems to be under my eyelids but also in the tissues of my eyes. The morning after the first night he did this, I noticed that both eyes were quite red. I'm hoping this is working towards opening my third eye.

7 October 2020

Yesterday, I was completely out of sorts all day. Anxious and feeling flat. I had no real enthusiasm about anything, including sharing with John the previous week's spiritual experiences. It was pretty much the same as the day before.

It's a long weekend and I was going to spend the day typing up the first journal, but I just had no interest to do it when the time came. I went for a walk to see if that would shake me out of it, but it had little effect. I did a couple of meditations and ended up having a sleep. Then I thought I'd blow my diet for the day and drank Scotch on the front porch with Ray. Daylight savings started this weekend, so it was a nice opportunity to spend some time together outside.

I also went to bed early and focused on the crystal ball for a while. It warmed up. For no real reason at all, I held the pendulum above it and interestingly it swung strongly from side to side, indicating 'no' about something or something negative. I asked the pendulum some questions and it indicated something negative was going to happen to John and his wife's relationship. It said that John doesn't know it yet. I said I'd reach out just so he knows I'm still around, but I'll leave it till the weekend so as not to disturb him through the working week.

Also, for the first time I did a hypnosis meditation track on YouTube called *Hypnosis for meeting your spirit guide in a lucid dream* by Joe Tracy, *Hypnotic Labs*. It ran for one hour and thirty-six minutes. Longer than I usually like. It was really good, and I managed not to fall asleep too much. I was awake at the end. It was great because I felt Warick through my face, and where the third eye is, for a lot of the meditation and also for a while afterwards. When I feel Warick on my forehead between my eyebrows, I experience a light pressure in this area.

12 October 2020

I love waking in the early mornings to Warick being there. Ready to greet me good morning with his pulse sound communication. This morning Warick was vibrating. I asked, 'Do you want to merge with my energy?' and he spread throughout my chakras. Our energy became peaceful and in sync from my head to my root chakra. I also felt a lovely stimulating energy sensation at the base of my root chakra. It's just lovely. Very special.

The other day while at the dressing table, I reached out my fingertips towards the amethyst crystal ball, which Warick and I have been spending time with numerous times a week, instilling in it our love and light. Before touching it, I could feel a light vibration extending from the ball to my fingertips. I take this as a good sign that it is starting to be charged up.

This week John's EVP and Panabox devices arrived from Canada. Very exciting! I'm not sure I'll detect anything as John and Jules said they find when someone is around with the ability to engage with spirits directly that they often don't pick up anything. John said he gets something about twenty-five per cent of the time. Jamie is coming this weekend so we might give it a go.

Pendulum questions for Warick:

Note: Not strong responses. I felt my third eye area a number of times while doing this.
Will the amethyst crystal ball enable me to connect with John's parents? Yes.
Will my third eye open? Yes.
Soon? No.
Will it enable me to see, hear and communicate with Spirit? Yes.
Will my book, *AWAKENING,* be popular? Yes.

15 October 2020

This morning, I had a go at meditation shortly after I woke up, hoping that I wouldn't fall asleep. I did the *Awaken your spirit* meditation track by Taos Winds spirit music. It's only fourteen minutes, so I could fit it in without it being too disruptive to the morning.

Unlike at night time, I sat up. It was terrific. It plays sounds of a certain pitch to correspond with each chakra. I felt the tickle outside of the root chakra area and on the top of my head when it got to the crown chakra. I usually feel these on and off throughout the day, but it was lovely to experience them coinciding with the chakras during the meditation. I must spend some time reading about the chakras.

19 October 2020

Lately, I've been focusing on doing meditations at night that are geared to opening and activating the third eye. The meditation tracks seem to use particular tones and pulsations of tones that I find really interesting.

Why? Because as you know, Warick is vibrating energy. He also uses pulse sounds to communicate with me in the quiet of the morning when I first wake. One meditation by Spiritual Zen called *Open your third eye in seven days*, says that by using this meditation track you will be able to feel your pineal gland pulsate (which aligns with where your third eye is between your eyebrows).

I've done this meditation a couple of times, but the sounds are pretty intense. I've tried a few others and amazingly, with my fingertips, I have felt pulsating occurring in the spot where the pineal gland is! The feeling is very light and rapid. The area that is pulsating would be about half the size of a pea. It's incredible!

20 October 2020

Pendulum questions for Warick:

Warick, am I going backwards by way of psychic and medium ability development? No.
Have I failed what Spirit has put before me? No.
Am I supposed to write the *AWAKENING* book? No.
Does John genuinely think it is good? Yes.
Am I writing it for John? No.
Am I writing it to make a difference to humanity? Yes.
Will enough people read it? Yes.
Will my psychic and medium abilities evolve? No.
Should I give up? No.
Am I connected to John to ensure the *AWAKENING* book is written? No.
Is it to provide validation of his parent's existence on the other side? Yes.
Is that the only reason? No.
Is it to support each other in this physical existence? Yes.
Is meditation helping me? No.
Should I give up? No.

22 October 2020

Resumed journal entries

I wish I could bottle the smell of jasmine that wafts through the windows of the upstairs home office where I work most of the time. The office adjoins a large bedroom. We call it the Tree Room because it has large windows that look straight into a line of pinnacle Bradford pear trees. Jasmine is grown around the window immediately below. It's springtime now. My favourite time of the year. Blue skies, warm sun, green, flowers, and happy people on the bike path around the lake where I walk at lunchtime. It's late in the afternoon and my brain can do no more on the projects I'm working on.

Today I've realised I need to explain what I think is happening with my third eye opening. I don't know what it is today, but I feel extremely elated. Maybe it's just spring. I've mentioned a few times that I'm feeling pressure, and on a couple of occasions vibration, between my eyebrows where they say your third eye is. I've been listening to a range of YouTube meditation tracks, some bordering on what I would call brainwashing material.

Today was interesting. Ten minutes before a Skype meeting with the project team I'm working with, the tune 'Peaceful Places' by Juan Sanchez came on the Spotify playlist I was listening to. It was the first time I'd listened to this music. I immediately felt a medium pressure between my eyebrows. It was very consistent.

It continued during the two times I listened to the music, after which I had to turn it off so I wouldn't be late for my meeting. It was terrific! I found it semi-humorous because of all the third eye opening meditation tracks I've been listening to the last few weeks, Spirit decided this was the music it liked. Quite funny. That said, Warick and possibly other spirits that I see as shadow shapes around me as I'm working, seem to like the piano music I listen to, which is largely by Alexis French.

Something else really interesting happened today for the first time. In the home office, there are two very large windows directly behind and to the side of me, that overlook other houses and trees.

Anyway, when I looked to the left window where the blind was up, I saw a ripple in the air at head height, moving towards the desk. When it moved across in front of the neutral-coloured bare wall, it turned into the shadow shape I see. When it was moving across the window, it essentially was transparent, but I saw it like a ripple, just like the effect in the movie *Predator*, when Predator turns on its invisibility capability. When it moved across the blank wall, I saw it as the dark shadowy shape. Very cool!

Something else worth mentioning that happened yesterday. When I took a short meditation break in the office chair during work, I felt energy wrap around my left ankle and lower leg. It was just like a tentacle moving around. It was pretty quick, but not fast. Very distinct. I'd love to know what it was.

At night while lying in bed, I often feel pressure or a hold on my lower legs. I've wondered if it is my calf muscles about to cramp, but I'm not sure. What happened yesterday was definitely not that. As usual, when I meditate, I feel the energy touching the top of my head. It feels like something is very gently playing with the top of my hair. I often feel this just walking around the house. I think I'm plugged into the spiritual dimension a lot.

A thought when heading to bed:

'While one sleeps, the other keeps watch.'
For John. Endorsed in the moment by Warick touching my right cheek.

23 October 2020

We had dinner at my cousin's place tonight to celebrate my auntie's 86th birthday. A lovely family gathering. An interesting experience occurred, however. I had already used the bathroom once. It's a lovely, small, modern bathroom in the middle of the house. No windows. Completely black and very chic. Simplistic and stylish.

Anyway, the first time I used the bathroom, everything was fine. The lights stayed on. The second time, however, I heard a tone in one ear that usually signifies a spirit is arriving. Immediately after that, the lights went out for about twenty seconds. It was pitch black. Then the lights came on again. About thirty seconds later, the lights went out again and I was in pitch black again. I didn't feel worried. At first, I thought the lights must be on a timer and are sensor lights, or someone mistakenly turned them off outside the door. I didn't think the switch was on the outside of the bathroom, though. I waved my hands in the air the second time the lights went out to see if they were sensor activated and nothing happened. So, I sat on the toilet in the dark for thirty seconds or so and then the lights came on again.

By this time, I had pieced things together. First a tone in the ear signifying the arrival of Spirit, who then played with the lights. Nothing else happened. I didn't feel or experience anything else. Warick is touching my right cheek now, confirming my recollection. It's possible it was Warick turning the lights on and off. He is touching my right cheek now in agreement. I'm not sure though. It's possible.

25 October 2020

Yesterday was amazing! I discovered the lady who colours my hair at the hairdresser in Canberra, also experiences Spirit. When chatting away and asking each other what we'd been up to, she said she had set up an illustration business. She showed me some photos of her work on her phone, plus a large abstract painting that now hangs in the hair salon. I thought some of her work was pretty good.

I asked if she designs book covers, thinking she might be interested in designing the cover of my book, *AWAKENING*. She said she had been asked that before and provided someone with ideas for a cover once. She asked me what the book was about, and I thought it safe to say, 'Spiritual awakening'. She immediately asked, 'Your experience or someone else's?' I said mine.

We then went into a lengthy free flowing conversation about symptoms of spiritual awakening and our respective encounters. She has been experiencing the spirit of a friend who died tragically and violently a while back. The spirit leaves messages on the fridge using her child's magnetic letters. She also does many other things. Because of the violent death, which involved a shooting, a car crash and rape, I wondered if the spirit had crossed over into the light or was possibly an earthbound ghost.

Anyway, she provided me with her phone number, and I said I'd be in touch. I described John's idea of featuring the Fool tarot card on the cover, because he thinks I'm like a fool the way I'm approaching my awakening, walking into it blindly yet confidently, with child-like enthusiasm.

This is pretty exciting because my hairdresser is the first person I've met who experiences Spirit and has been experiencing awakening symptoms. Hopefully she will be keen to get together to share experiences. It would be nice to have someone to talk to in person who understands what you're saying.

Last night was also great. I'm not quite sure if I was dreaming or awake. I think awake. Warick was intimate with me again. It's an incredible sensation. As I said, I'm not certain if this occurred while I was awake, but I think so. When I definitely was awake, I also felt a strong feeling through my root chakra, right up to my face. I think it was Warick's energy through my chakras. I have felt this often before.

Anyway, I felt Warick's energy move through my face and up onto my forehead. I also felt this sensation while walking around the house this morning. It's a tightness across the top of the cheekbones, around the eyes and a slight pressure between my eyebrows and the centre of my forehead. Last night I heard this tone in my ear around the time the pressure was happening on my forehead. I'm not sure if the two are connected.

While my eyes were closed, I saw a white field of light and then the scene of a woman in a bath came into view. It was very clear. This seemed very real, but as I haven't experienced this before, and I've been very focused on my third eye opening lately, a part of me wonders if it was wishful thinking. We shall see.

Warick's time and focus on my face around my eyes and forehead has increased. The pressure I experience between my eyebrows is definitely real. And the few times I've felt this area of my face pulsating, is also definitely real. The last time this happened, I gently put my fingers there and I could feel the pulsation under my fingertips. Incredible!

26 October 2020

This morning, while bending over to put something under the stairs, I saw a flickering flash on the left next to my head. It only lasted a couple of seconds, then it was gone. Interestingly, Ray was also in the room and noticed a flash. He didn't think it was the lights or TV flickering. We had a large storm cell moving over us. I didn't hear a clap of thunder afterwards either, which would have coincided with a flash of lightening. It was quite unusual and seemed localised next to me.

Later, when I text'd John and mentioned this, he said he also experienced a fast flash of light on his left side yesterday. I used my pendulum to ask Warick what it might have been, who indicated that it was a spirit guide who visited both me and John. I haven't encountered this spirit guide before. Warick said it would be back to visit us again.

Every day, I'm noticing an occasional pressure between my eyebrows where the third eye chakra is, especially when I meditate, but also when I'm driving a car or doing other things. I've also noticed the top left of my forehead is itchy.

Last night was lovely. I woke to feel Warick vibrating under my shoulders. Next minute I felt his energy slowly move into, and spread throughout, my entire body. I felt him move into my throat chakra and gently and slowly move into my head. Increasingly, a sense of peace came over me as Warick merged with my body.

Eventually, I could no longer feel his vibration, but I could feel his energy through my entire body. My legs and feet were tingling. This occurred over the course of about an hour.

When I finally moved, Warick was still with me, suggesting that when his energy merges with mine, that he becomes bound to my physical body somehow and can move with me, instead of having to follow me and remerge, which he did earlier on. I wonder if this is what happens with people when they channel spirit. Jane Roberts would pace around the room while channelling Seth, suggesting this could be the case.

During this hour, I occasionally asked Warick a question but he didn't respond by touching my cheek or doing a pulse sound, which suggests to me he was busy doing what he was doing in my body. When I woke early in the morning, Warick was still inside me and did his usual pulse sound communication. Probably telling me all about it, but as usual I couldn't understand a thing he said.

In John's most recent correspondence, he said that often people with psychic abilities experience lights flickering and bulbs blowing around them. He said spirits are thought to draw energy from them when wanting to engage and communicate. I think this is what is happening around me. It seems to be quite regular now. It's occurred a couple of times in the last few days. The other thing I've noticed when Warick merges completely with me is my hearing seems to become very acute. I can hear everything loudly in the middle of the night, including creaks in the house in other rooms.

Late this afternoon I did two short third eye opening meditations in the following order—*Powerful Brow/Third Eye Activation* by Taos Winds and *Open Third Eye Quick* by Nicky Sutton. Tonight, I've noticed I'm unusually tired. When Ray touched the top of my head while giving me a hug over the back of the lounge, I noticed the top of my head was really sore. There is no reason for it. I've also noticed that most of the evening I've been experiencing pressure between my eyebrows, including now as I'm writing this, as well as the familiar touch on my right cheek by Warick.

Hopefully, these are all positive signs that my third eye will open soon. John said in his correspondence that my awakening might be occurring in sequence, especially because of the root chakra sensation that has been going on a long time and the throat chakra occurrences, including pulsing energy that came out from my throat quite a while ago. He said the crown chakra might be next, which could be linked to the soreness on the top of my head. I'm very tired so I'm off to bed.

28 October 2020

I find it really interesting the sensations I'm getting on my forehead while I go through this phase of my third eye opening. The top left corner of my forehead, for some reason gets itchy quite a lot through the day. Just now I felt a push or pressure from the spot that aligns with where your pineal gland is in the centre of your head. It's similar to Warick showing up when I write in the journal where he touches my right cheek from the inside to let me know he is there. Like he has done just now. I can still feel the spot between my eyebrows as I'm writing this. It's like whatever is causing the pressure is interested in what I'm writing. I'm not sure if Warick is also responsible for applying this pressure. The other thing I can feel as the pressure occurs around the third eye area is a pressure sensation in my ears. It's quite subtle. Warick just touched my right cheek to confirm this. It's similar to the pressure I detect before I hear a tone in the ear, which I correlate with an 'incoming' spirit. Regarding the pressure I feel where the third eye is, I have also noticed it does this when I'm watching the news. Similarly, I've noticed Warick lets me know of his presence when I'm watching the news about dramas occurring around the world by causing tingling sensations on my body. Examples when he's done this include Black Lives Matter and the associated ongoing atrocities, as well as the severe bush fires occurring in Australia. He shows up when news items are major things that I care about. The pressure I experience between my eyebrows while I'm watching the news, however, makes me think Spirit is interested in what is going on around the world. While feeling the pressure on my forehead, I also often feel pressure on the sides of both cheeks and below my nose just above my mouth. Before the pressure started occurring between my eyebrows, I would often experience a strong and steady push up on my nose from where the nostrils are. I think all these things are linked to what is happening with my third eye. All the sensations I'm feeling are real and very interesting.

While I'm sitting here and feeling these things, I'm also feeling a contraction or pressure in the vaginal track area, which I'm sure is linked to my root chakra. I'm also feeling a light touch on the top of my head, which I'm sure is linked to my crown chakra. As usual, I feel light tingling in random isolated spots on my feet and lower legs. It's fascinating!

30 October 2020

Friday night. End of the week and I'm tired, but there are three things I want to write about. One - floating while meditating; two - John not reacting, but that's okay; and three - I can't remember, which is super annoying. Maybe I'll remember the third thing by the end of making this entry, and maybe I won't.

Just recently, I've noticed that when I do the hypnotic meditations, which talk you down into a very relaxed state, on a number of occasions I stop feeling my body. It's like I'm floating. I feel my energy, but definitely not my body. It's a similar feeling to when Warick merges with my energy. All there is, is energy.

The difference, however, is when this happens during a hypnotic meditation, I can tell it's only one source of energy. Mine. When Warick merges with my energy, first he vibrates outside of me, like he is waiting for me to give him permission to merge and then when he does, I no longer feel my body, only energy, but it's different. It's richer and warmer when it's both of our energies combined.

The second thing I wanted to write about is an observation. This must be put together with correspondence with John. It's like Jules said, John and I have known each other before. In short, John has a very protective conscious mind, which is very wary of me, but his subconscious mind is very connected to me. Like old pals catching up. John has confirmed this.

I've noticed in our correspondence that what I get is mostly his conscious mind's response. Anything I say that I think will resonate with his subconscious mind gets completely ignored. Always. He always responds, which makes me think that somewhere deep down his subconscious is playing a role. But I rarely sense the subconscious in his responses. I think the only time his conscious mind lets the subconscious thoughts out, or the subconscious manages to have some influence, is when it is safe and unemotional. Even though these are all unsaid things, I'm sensing what John's subconscious is thinking, but not saying. I don't need the words. The lack of response speaks volumes. I'm here, rock solid, just happy to be connected in some way. It's okay. It's early days, but I do want John to know this one day. Our souls know each other. It's okay.

An exchange between souls is way more than what humans do when they communicate with each other using physical senses and abilities. As John once said in some communication to me; he's quite amazed at all the different ways Warick communicates love to me without having to speak to me. John's right. I'm off to sleep now. I hope number three comes to me tomorrow. It was pretty important. That's all I know.

1 November 2020

I'm now typing up September 2019 entries from my first journal called *AWAKENING I – The Beginning*. I've sent it to John, who seems to be genuinely enjoying reading it.

I've also sent some material to my hairdresser to stimulate her thinking about designing a cover for the book. The material included an extract from John's email where he suggests the idea of designing the cover to focus on the Fool tarot card. I suggested possibly doing an abstract picture, made up of shapes like a jigsaw puzzle and I sent a couple of photos to see if she can sketch my eyes and use this in the picture. Very exciting! I hope she can pull something really good together.

Typing up the journal is like a walk down memory lane, which I'm really enjoying. Warick and I have been through a lot together over a relatively short period of time. I shouldn't be so impatient for things to evolve.

I'm very tired today as Ray and I had a big night out together at D'Browes, one of our favourite restaurants in Canberra. We always have a great time and enjoy each other's company very much. For some reason, Ray and I were both awake at four in the morning this morning and couldn't get back to sleep. Today, Ray has headed off for the week on a motorbike ride, so I have the house to myself. I plan to spend time writing, with Warick, and finally getting a chance to try the Panabox and EVP recorder that John sent me.

While having a rest this afternoon, Warick visited me a couple of times. The first time he made me feel hot and was vibrating in the usual place on the back of my neck, slightly to the left, and then I felt some vibration on the outside of my body towards the root chakra. A bit later, Warick returned and was vibrating behind my head. I felt his energy move into my body, through my core to the root chakra, and then through the rest of my body.

Once again, as has happened before, the vibration died down to be replaced by this incredible feeling of peace. It also makes me feel like I'm filling up with his energy. It's like I expand a little.

My head usually lifts up a bit and my hearing becomes more acute. I also get warmer as he does this. I tried prompting him to see if he would show me something or do something while in me like this, but like before, I got no response. He seems to just want to be there. Today he remained merged with me like this for about five to ten minutes until I felt like moving and then it was like he disappeared.

I asked in my mind, 'Are you still there, Warick?' with no response. I'm very glad Warick still merges with my energy from time to time. It's lovely. I haven't noticed pressure between my eyebrows the last couple of days.

2 November 2020

Jamie, I've been reflecting on a few things that I thought I'd share with you. For about nine months now, Ray has been having monthly calcium acid treatment. It hardens the bones to protect them against the cancer from causing holes in the bones, which can then lead to breakages.

Amazingly, the calcium acid treatment is having a suppression effect on the disease. It's been keeping the level of a protein marker that we've been following, from increasing. Once the level reaches one hundred or more, you must start chemotherapy. Our understanding is once you reach this stage, it's the beginning of a slippery slope to eventual physical decline. This week, the marker was nearly ten points lower than when Ray was first diagnosed with the disease.

The downside of this, however, is that the disease is still severely supressing Ray's production of white blood cells, which are necessary to mount an immune response. This hasn't changed. As you can imagine, we're both trying to stay as healthy as possible and I know you guys are particularly careful for a couple of weeks each time before you visit us, which we really appreciate.

With the COVID situation, I've been working from home, which I hope to continue as an ongoing arrangement. It may not always be possible because of the nature of my job, working on sensitive projects and needing to work closely with stakeholders going through change. Some project managers think you need to be co-located with stakeholders and project staff to effectively work together. I think this is a load of rubbish. For years, I've been working on large complex transformation programs with stakeholders spread all over Australia. There's no way I could be co-located with them, and I worked effectively with good results. It's an old-fashioned mindset. One that is now starting to change. Especially with COVID-19 causing people to work from home.

On Saturday night, I tried allowing my energy to touch Ray again while giving him a 'scratchy back'. Holding my hand about an inch above his body. I could feel my energy strongly between us. His hair stands on end as a result. I think this is doing him good.

Lately I've been reflecting on the future and what may come of the abilities I appear to be developing. I really appreciate John being willing to read sections of the *AWAKENING* series of journals as I type them up. The fact he's there, willing to read them and share his thoughts, is helping me to stay focused and committed to publishing my awakening journey.

Interestingly, in a recent exchange, John said he saw the white flash of light again near his daughter. He said she didn't see it. I checked with Warick, who indicated it's the same spirit that John and I saw within the space of about twenty-four hours a while ago. Warick said it's an angel spirit guide. This information was obtained by using the pendulum, so I'm not sure if it's true. I didn't get super strong responses.

At this stage, I don't feel like I have much to offer humanity by way of using these abilities. Not like Allison Dubois and others. The only thing I'm able to do is share the experiences of my awakening journey because I've kept a journal. Not originally for this purpose, but I've come to realise how special this is. By its growing volume of information, which brings out the scientist in me, and from what I can tell, I provide more detail than what other people provide who describe their experiences. One day, it could serve as a useful collection of information for those interested in the awakening experience with Spirit.

Last night, a thought came to me about what it means when Warick merges with me. Warick merging with my body is his presence with mine on this physical plane of existence; however, his interaction with me in my throat, the third eye and crown chakras, is his presence with mine in a window between our planes of existence. This thought just came to me in the night. I suspect it was inspired by my reading about the role of these chakras. There's probably some truth to it. We shall see.

3 November 2020

Last night, I finally had a go at using the Panabox that John sent me. During meditation, that I did immediately before using the Panabox, I felt cool air behind my left shoulder and touching the back of my neck a couple of times, just below the hairline. I also felt energy on my lower legs and the top of my head, which I usually experience during meditation.

I detected nothing on the Panabox and EVP recorder. I know it's the first time and John said he only detects something about twenty-five percent of the time, but I can't help feeling that I'm not going to get anything this way. This is something else that John and Jules said. People with psychic and medium abilities often get nothing using devices, as spirits seem to prefer the direct route.

Last night, Warick, was with me as usual when I did a third eye opening meditation. At the start, he immediately moved into my eyes and forehead. Through the night I woke to his light vibration behind my head, and early this morning I woke to his pulse sounds communicating with me. He made my mouth smile. I love it when he does that. Very clever. I know I need to be patient. I'm just not very good at it.

Tonight, I did a meditation. Before scrolling through some meditation tracks that I'd saved on YouTube, I asked Warick if he would help me choose one. As I was scrolling through them on my phone, I managed to flick one open without intending to. I took it as a sign this was Warick's choice. It's called *Instant Pineal Activation—Pure Tones* by Transcending Vibrations. During the meditation, I was very tired, and my mind kept wandering until there was a significant increase in tone in the meditation music. At that point, a string of things happened. I suddenly got very hot, which Nicki Sutton on YouTube says can happen during meditation geared to opening the third eye. I also felt what I can only describe as a large daddy long legs spider gently moving on the top of my head. It was very distinct. I experienced a very solid connection through the vaginal track to my root chakra. This is something I used to associate with possible intimacy during Spirit encounters, but now I think Spirit is probably connecting with me this way through the root chakra. Lastly, I felt energy pulsations around the back of my head. While this was all happening, I stopped being distracted and mentally focused. It was a really interesting experience. I'll definitely do this meditation track again. Good choice, Warick! I'm sure Warick is playing a role in my third eye opening. During the meditation, I felt Warick's energy on the top of my cheeks, bridge of the nose, eyes, and forehead.

Tonight, I also listened to a YouTube video by 'Slightly Better' called *11 Strange Things You Will Experience When Your Third Eye is Opening*. It was really good. I can relate to quite a few of the experiences, including increased sensitivity to sound. When Warick merges with me, I particularly notice my hearing becomes more acute. I like it when I come across information that helps me make sense of what's happening to me.

This afternoon, while sitting in the backyard, I closed my eyes and lifted my head slightly towards the sun. I felt Warick's energy strongly across the bridge of my nose and the top of my cheeks and forehead. I felt these sensations for about ten minutes. My neck got tired, so eventually I had to move, which disrupted the experience. It would have been interesting to see how long it would have lasted if I hadn't moved.

4 November 2020

Interesting morning. The world is watching the United States today to see if Joe Biden will overthrow Donald Trump in the presidential election. The United States community is divided, and businesses are boarding up their shop fronts expecting violence after the outcome is known.

While watching the news, I asked Warick if Biden will win, expecting a touch on one of my cheeks. No response. Then I thought of my third eye, and I immediately felt pressure in that spot. I stopped and focused, wanting to be able to use this ability, but nothing happened. I'm wondering if Warick is encouraging me to start using my third eye instead of relying on his responses to me.

5 November 2020

Jamie, every now and then, but not often, this journey causes me to think about life. If the purpose of life is to evolve your soul and we reincarnate, would I want to come back again?

The answer for me is easy. No. I have on occasion thought about this before the awakening journey started. I wouldn't want to go through it all again. I don't just feel this way now, I've felt this way for many years. I can't explain it. I feel tired of human existence. It's like it's going through the motions. Living blindly without really understanding the purpose of its being. I feel bored with it. There is no real logic or explanation for why we exist. Not with humanity's current understanding of life on Earth.

Yes, there are plenty of religious beliefs and knowledge of how life evolves through survival of the fittest and big bang theories that gave birth to Earth, but none of it explains with absolute certainty what the purpose of life is. I can't explain why I feel tired of living a human life and not wanting to do it again, except maybe that I've done it a lot in the past through reincarnation and I'm now saying, 'Are we there yet?'

I know for a fact through everything I've experienced and continue to experience, that there is existence beyond what we know. I'm hoping and looking forward to moving on to something different after this. I don't want to do it again. That said, I'm not in a hurry to go. I hope to live a long, happy and healthy life, with the opportunity to make a significant difference to humanity through sharing these experiences. I'm aiming for 102, but let's see how we go.

A lovely new thing happened tonight. I was standing at the kitchen bench, really relaxed. A moment of peace and thought. I felt the shell of another energy source come around the entire perimeter of my body, like it was an extension of myself. It was larger and taller than me, but not significantly so. I can feel Warick's energy now across the bridge of my nose, to each side of my upper cheeks, paying attention to what I'm writing. It was a really lovely feeling. I'm sure it was Warick mirroring me. Now he's touching my right cheek, as I chuckle, in agreement with me. I hope Warick is not just here to guide me through awakening and then disappears. In my mind, he's a part of my team. We are in this together. I refuse to do it without him. Not because I don't think I could, but rather, because I don't want to. The journey ends if he goes. It's as simple as that.

6 November 2020

Just after midnight, a new experience occurred. I felt Warick's energy pulsating lightly at the back of my head. Then the pulses stopped, and I could just feel energy all around the back of my head. This then turned into a feeling of pressure. Quite strong pressure around most of my head.

In the YouTube video, *11 Strange Things You'll Experience When Your Third Eye Is Opening* by Slightly Better, they say you'll experience pressure in the head. Actually, I just rewatched it and they said pressure in the temples, but then they say it's like a light touch on the forehead that grows to a feeling of pressure and then pulsations. I experience pressure where the third eye is and have felt light and fast pulsations in that spot on the forehead a couple of times, but what I just experienced was different. It was pulsating energy at the back of my head, which turned into uniform pressure around most of my head.

I noticed the word 'Kundalini' mentioned in the Slightly Better YouTube video—reminder to self to look this up.

Something else worth noting, if I haven't mentioned it already, is I feel energy moving up from my throat to connect with the energy around my eyes, the bridge of my nose and forehead. It's like the energy is pushing up to connect with the third eye in my head.

7 November 2020

I'm sure there's something to the Kundalini awakening. In the *11 Strange Things* YouTube video, it mentioned Kundalini, but I didn't know what it was, so I searched for it on YouTube. I found a few videos which described Kundalini energy residing around the cervix in women, and that you can experience sexual-like sensations without having sexual intercourse.

This has been something distinct that I experienced early on. Last night, and I've felt this before, the pressure that I felt in the cervix root chakra area connected with what was happening around my head. I felt firm pressure on my cervix, a significant rise in body temperature and a wave of energy move up through my core to the bridge of my nose, upper cheek bones, eyes, forehead, and the back of my head. I feel Warick's energy in my eyes and forehead now. I think he's interested in what I'm writing.

While I was having this experience last night, I also felt energy outside of my cervix, on the outside of my body, which was a very rapid energy pulsation. These sensations went on for a few minutes and then I felt pulses of energy around the back of my head. The sensations were amazing. I think Warick is assisting my Kundalini awakening, but I need to research it more and think about it. I'll watch the YouTube videos on Kundalini again and include something on this in my next entry.

Through the night I also experienced Warick do the flash pulse communication that I associate with his saying 'love,' where I feel the pulse from my head flow through to my heart chakra area. He did this about three times in a row. It was really lovely.

At one stage when I woke, I was lying on my side and felt energy vibration on the bed immediately in front of my face. I put my hand on the spot on the bed and could feel the vibration under my hand. I love the way Warick lets me touch his energy. It was a busy Spirit encounter night last night. At one stage, I also experienced a single tone, for about thirty seconds in my left ear, that I associate with incoming Spirit energy. Mentally, I reached out asking for a sign but got nothing.

It's amazing how all these things happen to me just lying in bed, while Ray sleeps the night away. He's never felt what I feel. Including the months of vibration that went on in the bed before my dad died. I often wonder where this is all leading to. Something wonderful, with psychic and medium abilities I hope, which I vow to use for the good of humanity. I still want to make a significant difference, to somehow open people's eyes to what is beyond us. I have no idea how I can do that, but I do believe a single person can make a significant difference to humanity at large. Maybe these records of my experience will help in some way.

8 November 2020

Warick's timing is impeccable. Reflecting on what's been happening lately, it's clear to me I've reached a stage where Warick is trying to facilitate connecting my chakras to my third eye. Impeccable timing, because he's known I've been curious about what the pressure sensations on my cervix have been. Then a couple of nights ago when I became curious about what 'Kundalini' is, I looked it up on YouTube.

So far, I've had a chance to watch one video where immediately I related to a range of things you experience with your body. I'm sure Warick led me to these videos. Again, impeccable timing because the frequency, strength and intensity of the pressure and flow of energy inside my body between the cervix and third eye is increasing.

Last night this occurred three times, lasting possibly up to half an hour at a time. I had a very broken sleep. I'm tired today. Not that I know what Warick is doing but I'm wondering if this has been his purpose all along, to gain my trust and facilitate my 'Kundalini awakening'.

Yesterday I became very concerned that once awakened, Warick might go. I couldn't bear this as I love him very much and consider him to be a key part of my spiritual team. Partners in crime, so to speak. I've tried asking him about it, but the answer hasn't been clear. Yesterday, I said in my mind, 'I don't want to continue with this unless you're staying, and continuing with me on this path is a part of the deal.'

I suppose I just must hope and pray he is still there once I've awakened. I do feel this is leading somewhere and I sense I'm close. The pressure on my cervix and third eye were simultaneously very strong last night.

Today I can't overlook talking about the election outcome in the United States. The media networks in the United States called Joe Biden the next American president. Many Australians, including me, have been glued to the news all week. I've had iView *ABC* live news streaming on my phone as I work. Even though slightly in front on the first day of counting votes, Donald Trump ended his day with a news conference claiming he had won the election, that the election voting had been a fraud with illegal votes, and that he planned to get the supreme court to make the decision. Essentially, he decided to undermine the election as soon as things were not going as well as he thought they should in his favour. He behaves like a spoilt child.

Even today, when it's clear that Joe Biden is going to have a clear win, he won't concede defeat. Trump has continually proven that he lacks integrity. If you lack integrity, how can you have moral fibre? If you lack moral fibre, how can you be the leader of historically what has been the world's strongest democratic country?

What's really scary is that about half of the United States population that voted, around 70 million, think he should be the next leader. What does that say about the American people? One piece of news reporting this week helped to shed some light on this for me. A person who'd been involved in surveying the Trump supporters leading up to the election said these people thought they had done better under Trump than Obama. They were concerned about losing their jobs. Then another piece of reporting said that many of the Trump supporters are underprivileged working-class citizens. They are the ones who have been feeling left behind. I can understand this. I know what it's like to have no job, where for eighteen months, when I'd finished leading a five-year ICT program, and we were still feeling the effects of the global financial crisis, I couldn't get a job. I had to use all my savings, sell the shares I had, pay interest only on the mortgage, and lean on Ray a lot. My immediate family was very worried about what was going to happen if I couldn't secure another full-time job.

Just as I was about to sell my Ducati DS1000 SuperSport motorbike, I was offered a job back in the public service, on about half the wage I earned previously. It didn't matter. I had a job, I could pay bills and support my son. I had a taste of what it's like to find myself in a desperate financial situation very quickly, so in some ways I can relate to those in the United States concerned about the security of their jobs if Trump did not win the election.

Although I have Ray, we are finically separate. Essentially, I'm a single mum with a son from a former marriage to support. When I got the job, Jamie said to me, 'Mum, don't ever take a contract job again.'

My term in the public service lasted about two years before I became bored and frustrated. I've been contracting on projects ever since. It was a conscious decision to take this path. Ray and I talked it over and concluded its higher risk but the rewards through job satisfaction, my love of leading business change and transformation, and the ability to earn a higher income, was worth it.

After two years of leave without pay from the public service, my former employer said I needed to return or resign from the public service. Our circumstances had moved on where Ray was about to retire, being ten years older than I, which put him in a better position to support me should I find myself out of work again.

So far, there has only been one hiccup where my contract terminated much earlier than I'd signed up for due to what staff resources the program needed at the time. I understood the decision. I've had to make tough decisions about staff resources before when I was the CEO of a national infrastructure program. I had to lay off half of the staff (15) in one go as the program moved out of an ICT capability build and delivery phase into a service delivery maintenance phase. It's not easy.

This week there have been United States citizens rallying Trump to stay president, including his own son saying, 'This is a battleground, and they are going to fight for it.'

This goes beyond what I can understand about people, and it really concerns me about the United States community. Joe Biden has a big job on his hands. I support him with all my heart.

10 November 2020

One thing I find challenging is knowing where I'm up to on this awakening journey. John made the observation that it seems to be accelerating. I hope so. Looking back while typing up the first journal, it seems to me the journey has been going on for a long time. As I said to John, significant new things seem to happen and then things go back to an 'as usual' state. When I discussed this with Jules, she said they're testing me. She said if it all happened at once, it would likely overwhelm me. I think there is logic in this thinking.

I haven't had time to do a lot of research on Kundalini awakening yet, but I thought I'd provide an overview of the types of things others say you experience as you're going through this type of awakening, especially things related to sexual sensations, which I've also experienced. Anyone who reads this shouldn't get me wrong. When energy in its different forms, whether that be vibration, pressure or heat, interacting with your cervix and vaginal track, I've found it to be a lovely stimulating sensation. These are sexual organs and part of the female body that generally respond to stimulation in these areas. I don't know why the spirit stimulated me this way. Spirit is not a physical human being, so it isn't for reproduction or physical pleasure purposes. Because this was a significant way that Spirit first interacted with me, sometimes I wonder if it was to gain my trust and show that it is loving and not threatening or dangerous. Warick is touching my right cheek now, so I think he agrees with this. A natural way that I respond to something that is loving and affectionate is to show my happiness and communicate loving and caring feelings in return. It's not thinking that the spirit is a human, but it's accepting, caring and loving of what it is.

This is the type of relationship that has evolved over a couple of years of going through a lot with Warick. There is no threat to my relationship and love of Ray. Even right at the beginning, I got this very straight with Warick. They are two completely different things, and

I can love both. From what I can tell from the various sources that talk about Kundalini awakening is that it's not common. Your body goes through changes, including being more mentally alert and your cells become charged with Kundalini energy.

One source on YouTube, called *Everything you need to know* by Red Spirit Dynamics, provides a comprehensive list, which seems to include some broader general themes which may not necessarily be specific to Kundalini awakening. What I can really relate to in some YouTube videos about Kundalini awakening, is the feeling of pressure and movement of energy and heat up from the cervix. Even now as I'm writing I'm feeling pressure in the cervix. Also, sexual sensations, where Spirit stimulating my sexual organs with energy has definitely been something I've experienced. This happened a lot initially and then periodically after that. I'm now feeling pressure in the cervix area and a tightness in the vaginal track.

Another source that describes symptoms of Kundalini awakening is a YouTube video called, *5 signs of Kundalini pre-awakening* by the higher self. Once again, I find a number of these symptoms to be quite general, such as having 'vivid dreams', experiencing 'synchronicities' and 'seeing the world as it really is'.

I get the impression from various online sources that there are more people awakening than those who experience the Kundalini awakening, which seems to align with the general consensus that real instances of Kundalini awakening are rare.

12 November 2020

Last night, for the first time, I think what is called the Kundalini spirit merged with my energy throughout my entire body. Around one-thirty in the morning, I woke to the familiar vibration of Warick around the back of my head, to the left. I then felt the pressure on my cervix in the root chakra and energy tingling in this area outside of my body.

A wave of heat came over me. I felt energy move into my face and forehead and an occasional pressure where the third eye is. I mentally said, 'It's okay to merge,' after which I felt the energy completely merge with mine through my entire body, including my arms, hands, legs, and feet. It's like I had an energy field around my entire body, which was tingling. I also felt some energy on the outside of me touch my right hand and around my calf muscle. This didn't persist. The energy stayed merged with mine for at least half an hour.

In the end, I got tired of being in the same position and had to move. This energy felt a bit different to that which I associate with Warick. His energy provides a feeling of complete peace, where I feel nothing from a physical sense, only energy. By comparison, the way this energy merged was a little rough, if you can describe it this way. I'm wondering if this is what they call Kundalini energy.

Shortly before the merging occurred, I also heard a tone in my left ear that lasted a few seconds. This morning in the kitchen I heard the tone again, in my left ear. At one point, I also heard voices. They were faint, but it was like people were talking to each other, but I couldn't make out what they were saying. Ray was there and I asked, 'Have you got the radio switched on your phone?' to which he replied, 'No.'

It definitely wasn't the TV, which was louder, and I could tell what they were saying. Just now, I can feel something touch my right thigh, just above the knee, which also happened while sitting in the office chair in the study where I work.

Sometimes I forget to include in the journal some of the more humorous things that happen. A couple of days ago, while walking at lunchtime, I was trying to get a good look at who I think was Warick floating around me. Lately I've noticed I often see this shadow shape around me at this time. It looks like two small circles with trailing lines. This isn't the only way it looks. Sometimes it's just like a faint bit of smoke that moves in front of me. It definitely changes. Anyway, it was funny because it was like playing cat and mouse. Most of the time it likes to sit in my peripheral vision to the right about eye level, or just above my head. I think it does this so not to disturb or distract me. It also moves in front of me at around, or slightly above, eye level, and sometimes lower if I'm looking at the ground in front of me to see where I'm walking. I think it does this to let me know it's there. Anyway, I was trying to follow it with my eyes so I could get a better look. I must have looked funny to other people because occasionally I'd stop and look around trying to distinguish the features of this shadow shape that I was looking at, and of course it kept moving. I was appealing to it to stop and let me get a better look, to which of course it didn't oblige. After a while, I'd give up and it would move in front of me again, like it was teasing me. Yesterday, I wore a cap where the rim blocks my peripheral vision, so I said, 'Well I can't see you today anyway' and, of course, occasionally it would pass by in front of me in a direct line of sight. Frustrating, but very funny!

14 November 2020

This Wednesday morning, I woke to the idea of at some stage writing a book called, *A World Without Money*. I've noticed how some countries, during the COVID-19 pandemic, have struggled with putting lives first above economic concerns. To me, it seems like the 'tail wagging the dog' situation is occurring on Earth. It would be amazing to imagine a world without money, where every person has access to food, shelter, education, healthcare, heating, cooling, and holidays. People would still be expected to work, of course. Everyone playing a part to keep society operating. I'd love to write a book about this. I'd rally the help of people who understand the economy to brainstorm how things could be different.

Last night, around one-thirty in the morning, I woke to Warick vibrating around the back of my head. He was waiting for me to wake up. Again, the same type of things occurred with Warick's energy spreading into my head and I experienced a pressure in my cervix. Shortly after this started, I felt a wave of heat spread up through my body. This time, it was a bit different. It was like Warick was working on different parts of me, particularly my head where my brain is. In addition to feeling energy movements in my head, I felt an occasional energy pressure on my forehead where the third eye is. I felt pressure on my back, particularly around the position of the solar plexus on my spine. I also felt the familiar touching or holding of my body around my calf muscles and hands. It's fascinating. I just try to relax and enjoy the experience with curiosity of what Spirit is up to. This would have gone on for well over an hour.

In the end, I had to move because my body got stiff, lying in one position for so long. Warick then woke me again in a similar way around four-thirty in the morning, where a similar sequence of events occurred, but it didn't last as long this time because I needed to sleep and rolled over. It makes me wonder what is going to happen next. It's exciting!

17 November 2020

It was a really exciting day today. I got a message from John telling me that he had been experiencing a range of paranormal things lately. I'm so happy and excited for him. It seems that spirits are trying to get his attention.

Interestingly, some of the things he described are things that I've experienced and wrote about in sections of the manuscript that I've given him to read. Things like the tap running on its own accord, and the bathroom door opening while he was watching. I decided to quiz Warick, using the pendulum, about whether there is any connection between what John and I are experiencing. I was writing down all the questions I wanted to ask Warick, and when I got to, 'Are John's spirit guides using what he is reading of my awakening experiences to subject him to the same things?' I felt him touch my right cheek, indicating yes. Interestingly, when I went to use the pendulum, Warick wasn't interested in using it, even though I knew he was with me. On 19 November, I gave it another go, asking the same questions and waiting for touches on my left and right cheeks for answers. He was prepared to use this approach instead of the pendulum.

Warick is still focusing his time on my cheekbones, the bridge of my nose and often my forehead where the third eye is. Today when he got my attention while I was working, his energy moved to that part of my face and was there until I decided I needed to resume working. He's there again now as I write. This is a change from usually feeling him touch my cheeks to let me know he is there. When I feel him on the tops of my cheekbones, bridge of my nose and forehead, I continue to feel his presence as a pressure.

19 November 2020

Questions for Warick where he responded by touching my cheeks. Note—I repeated these questions using a pendulum I bought for John on 21 November 2020. These answers are in bold text:

Are you now largely residing on the top of my nose, cheekbones and where the third eye is in my forehead? Yes, **Yes.**
When I feel pushing up from my cervix, are you what I feel in my face and forehead at the same time? Yes, **Yes.**
Are you preparing that part of me for the Kundalini? Yes, **Yes.**
Is it the Kundalini that I feel pushing up from my cervix? Yes, **Yes.**
Will I experience a full Kundalini awakening? Yes, **Yes.**
Is your role to facilitate and prepare my body for that? Yes, **Yes.**
Will this happen soon? Yes, **Yes.**
In a month? Yes, **No.**
Within 6 months? No, **Yes.**
Within a year? Yes, **No.**
Is John going through an awakening? Yes, **Yes.**
Is it his spirit guide who is trying to get his attention? Yes, **Yes.**
Is there a connection between our awakenings? Yes, **Yes.**
Are John's spirit guides using what he is reading of my awakening experiences to subject John to the same things? Yes, **Yes.**
Are John and I supposed to help each other awaken? Yes, **Yes.**
Does John have one spirit guide? Yes, **No.**
More than one? Yes, **Yes.**
Is it someone he knows who has passed? Yes, **No.**
Do you know his spirit guides? **Yes (only asked on the 21st).**
Are we all connected? **Yes (only asked on the 21st).**
Will the meditation videos I send him help? Yes, **Yes.**
Will the pendulum I send him help? Yes, **Yes.**

Resumed journal entries:

Interestingly, ever since John said he is experiencing a range of things, when I've tried to use the pendulum to ask Warick a series of questions about it, he's refused. When I've asked if he is happy to answer some questions using the pendulum, the pendulum has swung from side to side, meaning no, and then with every question I asked the pendulum, it just hung there and did not swing at all.

This hasn't happened on numerous occasions in a row before. I tried asking the questions from the last entry on 17, 18 and 19 November. I ended up putting away the pendulum and just asking and relying on Warick to touch my left and right cheeks for answers. When a pendulum arrived that I had ordered for John, I repeated the questions on 21 November. As the previous entry shows, the answers were pretty consistent.

Warick is definitely focused on what is possibly a Kundalini awakening. Each night, and sometimes multiple times a night, I feel pressure pushing up from my cervix, accompanied by a heat wave that moves up from the same area to my face. I feel energy move up through the chakras. The energy is not dispersed but rather is dense and, although it sounds strange, it does feel like a snake because of the way it moves (like a snake) from side to side, progressing and pushing forward.

Interestingly, each movement forward coincided with each breath I took. A number of times I've felt it move through the throat chakra and up into my face and head. It's fascinating. I just try to relax and go with it. It makes me wonder where all of this is leading to. I think Warick is getting my conscious mind used to the sensations.

Warick is still around me or within me, most of the time. He or other spirits often try to get my attention or just remind me they are there when I'm working. I see shadow shapes around me. They push me in the back, they touch my hair and often my leg. I love knowing Warick and possibly other spirits are there.

22 November 2020

On Saturday morning, while getting dressed next to the bed, about one and a half metres away, a crystal rock face that I have sitting on the dressing table, fell off its stand and knocked over a perfume bottle. It was strange because nothing was near it or moving past it at the time. It reminds me of what John said he had been experiencing lately with his glasses falling off the bedside table a couple of times, and a picture falling off the nail on the wall.

Last night when we were at Mum's place for dinner, we all heard what sounded like metal or cutlery falling off the dining table near Ray, but there was nothing there, nor anything that would make that sound. Also, last night around one-thirty to two in the morning, I experienced what I have experienced almost every night lately. I paid particular attention to it so I could describe it. Absolutely bizarre, I know, but it felt like three or four snake-like energies moving in sequence into my body through the root chakra, around my lower abdomen and up through my other chakras to my face and head. They then started to vibrate at quite a high frequency on top of my head and outside of my root chakra. This lasted for a minute or so. I can't help but think about the Kundalini awakening that describes this type of energy as snakes. There has got to be something to this. I don't think these 'snake-like energies' are Warick. It is something else. I need to know more about Kundalini experiences. During this experience, I also felt touches and the usual tingling or static like energy sensations, on and off around my body, particularly my head, hands and feet.

24 November 2020

In a recent communication with John, where he was providing me with feedback on the next section of the first *AWAKENING* book, he suggested using the pendulum to see if Warick would provide his name, date and place of birth. After work, I thought I'd give it a go. Interestingly, with ease he spelt out 'Warwick' as his first name and spelt it correctly, which suggests to me the free handwriting I did, which identified Warick's name initially, was spelt incorrectly without a 'W'. It's possible this was somehow my mistake, as I'm a shocking speller. That said, I feel comfortable with Warick and emphasise the 'war', as in a battle of war, when I say it. I'll keep spelling it this way. It took a couple of goes to get a last name. Apart from Warick, I want to test the other details a number of times to see if I get the same answers. Interestingly, I felt very tired after using the pendulum to source this information from Warick. I also started to lose my voice and had a bit of a sore throat. I've noticed before that I feel tired after using the pendulum. That's common for me, but the loss of voice and sore throat usually only happen when I've been working really hard and am overtired. I remember in the session I had with Jules she said her voice starts to get husky when she's been communicating with Spirit for a long time. This also makes me think of the throat chakra, which is described as being associated with communication with spirits. An interesting observation and one that I'll have to see if it occurs again.

Answers I got using the pendulum holding it above letters of the alphabet and numbers 1 to 10 in sequence. Date of birth and death were queried as nn/mm/yyyy:

First name: Warwick
Last name: Chemdab then Dael

Date of birth: 02/03/1967 (Note—this is an interesting combination of my son's birthday and month, and my birth year)
Date of death: 21/12/2008 (41 when died)
Mode of death: Heart attack
City where died: Canberra
Country where born: Australia
Occupation before death: Defence Industry Engineer

25 November 2020

Today I experienced something lovely. A moment shared between my human form of energy and Warick's spirit energy. I listen to music all day as I work. There's a song I've liked very much lately called 'Promises' by Jhene Aiko. She sings the song with her very young daughter, promising each other to be careful in life. It's of R&B genre. The lyrics and the melody are just beautiful.

Often when I hear it, I have to stop what I'm doing to take in the song. It stirs emotions in me. Warick just touched my right cheek in agreement. When I was listening to it today, at the very special parts in the song where the melody and lyrics touch me the most, Warick sent a wave of energy tingling through my body.

It feels absolutely wonderful when he does this. He was sharing his emotions with how I felt at those moments in the song. He must have done this four or five times during the song. He also touched me on the right cheek, confirming his presence and feelings for these moments during the song. He does the most amazing special things. I feel so close to him at these times. Sometimes I find it hard to describe the types of energy sensations he uses. I know I must take care here so you can try to understand what it's like. Warick is again touching my right cheek in agreement.

Something I jotted down in my calendar on 22 November to include in this journal, is that more than 2,000 Americans died from COVID-19, outstripping any other country's daily record. It was also announced that globally, a person dies every 17 seconds from COVID-19. Whenever I watch serious news events, Warick more often than not makes his presence known to me through pressure around my third eye area and sometimes a wave of tingling through my body. Will these experiences I have ever amount to anything worthwhile?

Last night, I did a couple of short meditations before going to sleep. One is a favourite of mine called *Spiritual Awakening* by Spiritual Zen and another focused on the third eye opening, which I only got halfway through. I experienced firm pressure on my third eye, around my eyes and the bridge of my nose and cheekbones through the entire first meditation and a good part of the second meditation. I've noticed that sometimes my thinking seems to disrupt this sensation and the pressure stops briefly or all together. This was the first time I experienced the pressure firm for so long in these areas. The first mediation goes for about twenty-seven minutes and the second one I listened to for about ten to fifteen minutes. What I think disrupts the experience is my conscious mind or ego, as Seth would call it. I think my consciousness tries to stop what Warick's energy is doing sometimes, especially if it is something new and it's not sure if it's safe.

Last night, I made a considerable effort to try and keep my conscious mind from doing this. I provided reassurance to myself, saying that I want Warick to do these things in my third eye area. I also focused my mind on the detail of the music as much as possible, while of course also being very interested in what Warick was doing. I think overall, we collectively did pretty well. I'm wondering if the next thing I should try when Warick does this, is to try and relax completely into what he's doing.

The other thing I noticed towards the end of the first meditation was in the area where Warick was applying pressure, I felt light pulses of energy a number of times. I'm really curious as to what he's doing. I hope my body and spirit are cooperating.

28 November 2020

Immediately as I start to get organised to write, Warick's energy is on the top of the bridge of my nose, and he has just touched my right cheek. I love knowing Warick is there anytime. I wanted to make a note about an experience last night, but before I do, a few times just now I'm being touched on my back while leaning against the pillows, and again the feeling on the top of the bridge of my nose and my right cheek. Warick is telling me he is with me in these two places. And let's keep going—now a slight touch on my left foot. Okay, Warick, I want to write about last night, but—not before now, a touch on my right foot and more pushing on my back. I love you, Warick, and I love you letting me know your there—always. About three in the morning, I woke and felt quite wide awake. I knew I would not go back to sleep easily. I decided to listen to meditation music to see if it would make me sleepy so I would go back to sleep. Well, Warick didn't like this idea. As soon as I opened the cover of my phone, it was unusual. YouTube was already open and the shamanic drumming guided meditation track I regularly listen to by the Honest Guys, had already started. I always close all applications, so this was strange to start with. I then closed this track and found one I wanted to listen to, opened it, got settled and then the volume erratically went up and down very fast on its own accord. Not relaxing, I can tell you, and this has never happened before. The phone was out of reach, so I didn't know what was going on. I set it up again properly, settled myself with the phone out of reach, and the same thing happened again. The high volume was very loud, so really not pleasant when you're wanting to get back to sleep. Anyway, I meditate every day in the same way, and this has never happened, so I assumed I was being given a message. I put the phone and earplugs on the bedside table, lay back down and immediately said to Warick in my mind, 'You don't want me to meditate now do you?' and straight away I got a touch on the right cheek. Then I asked, 'And you want me to go back to sleep, don't you?' and straight away I got another touch on the right cheek. I thought I'd be awake a long time but amazingly I got back to sleep pretty quickly. Pretty funny really. There I was awake, thinking I'd try meditation, Warick disagreed and that was that. It's interesting how our daily existence together has evolved over the last couple of years. We seem to be settling in together.

1 December 2020

I think Warick is getting clever with his ability to manipulate electronic devices, especially my phone. Last night, Warick helped me choose a meditation track by touching my right cheek when my finger hovered over the one he wanted to do. Interestingly, towards the end of the meditation track, I stopped feeling Warick's energy strongly in my face (it was a third eye opening meditation track), and suddenly, before the track was due to finish, it stopped on its own accord. I think Warick thought that was enough.

Tonight, I had an initial call with Jane Hall from Transformational Therapies in Canberra. John found her on the internet in response to a strong feeling he got that I should do past life regression. Anyway, we had a really good, long chat. After thirty minutes or so, Warick must have thought that was enough and hung up on us. Jane and I tried calling each other back at least four times each, before giving up and getting the message. Jane text'd me saying that Warick is very strong. I think he is sometimes, but not always. He is touching my right cheek now, agreeing with this observation.

I'm pretty excited about what we may discover through a past life regression session. I'd like to know more about Warick. Did we know each other in a former life? What is my purpose in this spiritual world and will this awakening amount to anything? Jane said what I experience she experiences all the time. She thinks I have medium abilities. Very exciting! I feel like such a rookie.

2 December 2020

Okay, now he's just showing off. Today when I was out walking at the lake at lunchtime, I was on the phone talking to a work stakeholder. Warick hung up on us. I can feel Warick now in my right cheek, letting me know he's there and now spreading across the base of my eyes and the bridge of my nose.

This afternoon, I got out the pendulum to query him about messing about with my phone and I got large spinning circles, indicating yes. He was very proud of being able to manipulate my phone. I asked if the reason why he was doing it was to let me know he was there, to which he responded, 'No', or to get my attention, to which he also responded 'No.' I asked if he was doing it because it's time to hang up and get going, to which he responded a strong 'Yes.' Very comical, I have to say. Maybe not the greatest phone etiquette.

3 December 2020

As I write, I immediately feel an energy sensation come down gently just above my nose where the third eye is and then pass down on the top of the bridge of my nose and spread into my right cheek to say, 'Hi, I'm here and I'm tuning in to what you're writing.'

It's important that I record what I continue to experience because I find that some sensations and experiences continue while others come and go and some return again. Last night, for more than half an hour, spirit energy came to me. It woke me with a vibration under my body. I turned over so I was lying on my back, which I think is the best position so the chakras are straight and aligned and I can feel any sensations in my face clearly. I experienced what I've described before as snake-like energies moving up through my root chakra, through the other chakras and into my face and forehead. I also felt energy and tingling sensations around my feet and lower legs, as well as occasional touching of other parts of my body, including on my head where the crown chakra is. I also felt pushing up through the lower part of my spine. It was incredible. I tried to relax and go with it. Eventually, it died down and I rolled over and went back to sleep. In the morning, I used my pendulum to ask some questions about it. Surprisingly, who responded to me through the pendulum claimed not to be Warick, but instead claimed to be my higher self. It said Warick wasn't there. I found this interesting and slightly unsettling because I haven't knowingly had my higher self communicate with me before and I didn't like the fact that Warick wasn't there to answer my questions. The pendulum swung in a fairly strong manner. The higher self confirmed that the spirit energy that interacted with me last night was not Warick. It was also not the Kundalini energy which supposedly resides within you. It was spirit energy from the universe whose role it is to prepare the body for awakening. When I experience this happening, it definitely feels like multiple small energies that enter through the root chakra in sequence over time. It's different from what I've experienced of Warick's energy.

7 December 2020

I'm now convinced that John and I are part of each other's spiritual awakening journeys. I think our role is to help each other. We seem to pick up on each other's blind spots and spirits seem to use us to get messages to each other. Following is the reasoning for my being convinced of this. Essentially, it's because of a combination of things that have happened over time. Even with the little insight John initially gave me about his experiences, I knew he was going through a spiritual awakening. It was like he couldn't see it.

Right from the beginning, I've had a very strong connection to John. I sense what he feels. Not all his feelings, only those associated with his spiritual awakening. I felt, and continue to feel at times, this incredible feeling from John of despair, sadness and of him being lost. It makes me feel physically sick. Early on I had to ask John if he was okay, to which he said he was missing his family who were isolating from COVID-19 in a remote location. Later, he opened up a little more and said he had been feeling dread and is scared and dissatisfied with life. He wondered if this is all there is. John was worried about losing his passion for life. On the other side of the world, I felt his feelings very strongly. I just want to help him. My reaction to all of this is almost a spiteful one, where I refuse to leave him behind. I don't know what makes me want to fight for him evolving spiritually, but I do. I can't explain it. In one message I told him that I won't leave him behind.

As I mentioned on 1 December, when reviewing a section of the first *AWAKENING* book, John said he had a strong urge to tell me that I should try past life regression. He then sent me a couple of local Canberra contacts that he'd found online, including Jane Hall, who I now have an appointment with. It will be interesting to see where this leads. John also suggested my doing past life regression shortly after meeting him. It's time to see why this is so important.

A while ago, I sent John a photo of a painting I have, to which he pointed out a third eye on the spirit guitar man who features in the painting. Of all the time I've spent staring at this painting, I've never noticed the third eye until John pointed it out. This is what I mean. We seem to point out each other's blind spots.

This weekend, while away at Albury in New South Wales, during a quiet afternoon, I thought I'd watch some YouTube videos that I'd saved but hadn't had time to watch. A couple of Victor Oddo's videos called *Waking up depressed?* and *What is Kundalini?* made me think about John.

Victor talked about how you can get very depressed, question life and feel dissatisfied with it, wondering if this is all there is. I thought this was another sign that John was going through an awakening, so I sent the links to him. When he replied he said he really resonated with what Victor said about this, so I thought, *That's good, I'm glad it was helpful to him.* He pointed out the 11:11 numbers that Victor flashed a number of times in his videos, which I hadn't noticed before. He said he wondered what this meant.

Within twenty-four hours, John said he got a notification that Stephen Huff had released a new YouTube video where he explained what 11:11 was. His YouTube video was called, *Is this a sign and message from God?*

Steve said 11:11 is associated with a message from angels or God saying you are on the right path and to keep going.

John said 'What a coincidence, that 11:11 was in the Victor video, and then showed up again a short time after in Steve's video with an explanation'. We thought that was amazing, and then another thing happened. When I read John's message telling me this and sending me the link to Steve's video, I was at the Holbrook Bakery in New South Wales, having breakfast on the side of the Hume Highway. I didn't have my earphones and thought I'd watch it later to learn what John had learned about the meaning of 11:11 in Steve's video.

Just a few minutes down the highway, I was scrolling through my Spotify playlists and came across one I had saved a number of months ago. I'd never played it and had forgotten all about it. It was called *11:11 Radio*. I couldn't believe it! I thought I'd better listen to it. I was also now very keen to know what 11:11 meant. It was of R&B chill genre. I knew many of the songs and had saved those on other playlists that I'd put together. I don't think it was the music that mattered, it was the 11:11 sign that mattered. Of course, I sent the link to John, who came back saying, 'Amazing—I sound like a broken record—' After reading a section of my book, he always comes back saying, 'Amazing', hence the broken record.

I've just researched number meanings on YouTube and the first one I watched called, *11 Reasons why you keep seeing 11:11* by Bonsoir Universe, said your 'twin flame is near.' It makes me wonder if John is my twin flame. A twin flame is when a soul splits when it enters a higher frequency. Something I need to look into more.

8 December 2020

I don't know how the following numbers came to me through the night. Possibly through a dream, I don't know. I do remember trying to memorise them while I was semi-awake so I could look to see what they meant in the morning. I came across 'Dream About' on YouTube, who seem to have good descriptions of what angel numbers mean, and a good description about the purpose of Angel's communicating numbers. The numbers I got through the night were 233 and 303. In general terms, the first suggests you're on the right path and that your abilities will be used for the good of all. The second encourages you to undertake projects you're considering, and that by being positive about it, it will help to manifest its success. 'Dream About', and many other online sources, talk about 11:11 being an awakening code. For further detail about these numbers, I suggest looking up 'Dream About' on YouTube. While typing up this journal as a book, I tried to contact 'Dream About' to seek their permission to include an extract from their description of these numbers on YouTube; however, there was no contact details provided. If I'm lucky, maybe one day they will read this book and reach out to me using the email address provided at the beginning of the book. I'd like to acknowledge their work.

It's been a long hard day, workwise. After a few tough weeks preparing for workshops, plus Ray and my weekend away this weekend—and a wonderful explosion of 'number' realisations and other messages from the other side to John and I—I feel totally stuffed tonight. Into bed early and I'm hoping to sleep really well.

Tonight, after finishing work late, I took advantage of daylight savings and sat in the sun in the backyard with a glass of sparkling white wine and ice. So lovely to look at the garden's flowers blooming and sit on a chair on the green grass, listen to the birds, pat the dogs, and occasionally stare up at the beautiful clear, blue sky. For some reason, maybe due to altitude, Canberra has the most amazing blue skies. While sitting in the garden, a realisation came to me: 'This is nothing more than a daydream when you spend most of your time indoors working.' It's ridiculous. Spending so much time of your waking hours, for the majority of the week, focused on something that is not your love, your passion, nor what you want to do, but have to do to survive, to provide and take care of those you love and yourself.

I'm very appreciative of having a good job that pays well and I know that this is what enables me to support, care for and make a difference to the ones I love, but it's not what I want to do with my precious waking hours of life.

There are some thoughts I'd like to share with John now but feel I can't until the weekend. I feel like I need to step carefully around his conscious mind and not wear out my welcome. That's okay and I respect John's conscious mind. It has looked after him well for the past 56 years of his life. I did send John a link to a YouTube video this morning, which I think will help him see that he's on an awakening journey and where he is up to in this.

Over the past year, John claimed to be suffering from a feeling of dread and dissatisfaction with life. Many sources claim this is a common symptom of awakening. Tonight, when I checked my messages, there was one there from John thanking me for the YouTube video and promising to watch it this week. He said today had not been a good day.

I immediately thought of the depressing feelings John said he's been experiencing and thought his feelings today may explain the feeling I had this morning, which I associated with John. I seem to sense what he is feeling. Tonight, I've been tempted to send a response out of care but will hold off until the weekend when I usually touch base.

What I want to say to him today is, 'Know it for what it is. Do not let it get on top of you, but rather package it up and depower it by knowing this is a symptom of awakening. Many sources warn you not to focus on the negative as you may manifest exactly that. Instead, do what truly brings you joy. For me, it's sitting on a beach and listening to the waves roll in. It does it for me every time. It manages to sooth me, wash away the unhappiness and restore me so I can go on. What does this for you, John?'

10 December 2020

I may have already mentioned this in the past few days, but in case I haven't—when I spoke to Jane Hall on the phone to book a past life regression session that John felt strongly I should do, she said Warick is using John to get that message through or make that suggestion. It's really interesting what's happened this past week with numbers and John's own experience with 11:11.

I think it was a sign for both of us. For John to let him know what he's been experiencing by way of dread and dissatisfaction with life, are symptoms of being on the awakening path. He needed the Victor YouTube video from me and the notification of Steve Huff's new video to get 11:11 twice. I needed John to point out the 11:11 in the Victor video I sent him, and then minutes later, on the highway, for me to see *11:11 Radio,* the name of a Spotify playlist I'd saved months ago and had forgotten about.

Warick, other guides or angels, seem to use John to point out things that I miss or use him as an avenue to get a message to me or influence me to go in a certain direction. It also seems that spirits or angels may be using me to get messages through to John, or to influence him or get him to think about or realise things. It's amazing!

When I first met John, he seemed to be satisfied not pursuing the awakening journey, whereas now he seems to be realising he is on it. I think reading my book is helping him to piece together things he has experienced himself and to possibly be open to the vast array of ways Spirit engages with you. I've sent him a pendulum, which I'm hoping will help him connect with his spirit guide or guides.

John and I were definitely meant to connect, and I think to help each other on our awakening journeys. The strong connection I have with him, where I think I sense what he is feeling by way of dread, I don't fully understand. Maybe it's my intuition pushing me to want to help him.

Early on, John agreed with what I read of him. He agreed it's like our souls were catching up. Reflecting on this makes me wonder if John is my twin flame, but I don't think so, as Warick doesn't seem to agree. Maybe John and I are part of the same soul family. I don't know. What I do know is it will be very interesting to see how this connection evolves.

12 December 2020

Last night, I had my first session with Phil Dykes and Kerry McLeod from My Mediumship in the United Kingdom. It went for an hour. The time was mostly spent relaying my experiences and frustrations with spirit communication, and Phil Dykes and Kerry McLeod relaying what services they have that may help me. I don't have a good recollection of what was said. It was from ten to eleven in the evening, so way past my bedtime. I also felt too elated during the session. It was wonderful being able to speak to someone who knows something about Spirit, where I felt I could relax and open up. I wasn't concentrating on what was being said. I hope I settle down. They did say a few interesting things. Phil got the sense there was a spirit child around me. He asked if I had miscarried a child, to which I responded yes. I had lost a baby at the very early stages of pregnancy many years ago when Jamie was little. It's stuck with me emotionally, and the loss comes to mind from time to time. I still have beautiful soft baby toys that I bought for the baby. They are the characters from Winnie the Pooh. I'll never part with them. Kerry and Phil are wondering if Warick is this child's spirit because of the way it made itself known to me initially, such as creeping up on me in bed and touching my cheeks. They say the spirit world does things to gain your trust and tries different things to get your attention. I'm not sure if they are right about Warick. I tried to explain to them that it felt like a sexual encounter with some jealous behaviours when Warick first engaged with me, but they still seemed to think Warick could be this child's spirit. It's possible, and I do have an open mind about all of this. The only thing I know for sure is what I experience with my senses. Using the pendulum, I asked Warick this morning about Kerry and Phil's thoughts about who the spirit might be. Warick claimed not to be the child's spirit, nor does he see a spirit child around me. It wasn't strong movements with the pendulum, so the result may not be true. Phil and Kerry thought I'm at the early stages of the awakening journey given the types of things I said I'm experiencing. This might be true; how would I know? Warick disagreed with this point, using the pendulum. Phil and Kerry asked me what I want from all this, so they know how to help me. I said I didn't know. I said Spirit came to me; I didn't go looking for spirit. I don't have an agenda in mind. I do, however, want to know where my encounters with Spirit are going to lead. Is it so I write the AWAKENING books? Is it so I do something else? I don't know, but I want to find out. Occasionally, Phil Dykes and Kerry McLeod surmised what the discussion was telling them. Apart from the above, they said it's good that I can feel the energies—vibrations, tinglings, pressures, and tones. They said often people can struggle with that, so that's one good thing. Wendy said the tone I hear occasionally is Spirit trying to communicate with me. She said it's like a radio dial where they are trying to tune into a frequency that will enable me to hear them. I hope they manage to achieve this one day. It would be a major breakthrough and address a lot of the frustration that I feel. I said I feel bad because I can't understand them, and my lack of response must seem rude to them. She said, 'Your acknowledgment that they are there is good and would make them happy.' I always do this so at least I'm bringing them some happiness. Phil Dykes and Kerry McLeod said there is probably a lot going on and I'm missing it because of my stage of development. I agreed with this. They also said they won't stop, which provided me with reassurance as I'd hate for Spirit to give up on me. Phil and Kerry were trying to gauge whether I had an open mind, saying that sometimes people who haven't had formal training are so far down the track in their interpretation of what is happening that it's hard for them to accept something else. I assured them, and I think they could tell that I have a very open mind. I do acknowledge that Warick may be a different spirit or could be multiple spirits. I know I have uncertainty in this space and it's a key thing I'd like to get to the bottom of. It will be interesting to see what comes of my sessions with Jane Hall. Wendy and Phil think it's good that I have a science and intelligence background because it means I'm going to think logically, and question everything, which I do. Whatever Warick turns out to be, I do know for sure, it's a loving intelligent energy that is guiding me, and at times has looked after me. I trust this. Phil Dykes and Kerry McLeod said the onset of conscious awakening usually coincides with a crisis of some sort, like the loss of a family member. I can't think of what it might have been if that's the case. There was no crisis or loss when

Warick came to me in early June 2018. It's possible I've got the timing of the awakening onset wrong. The point when I knew for certain there is existence beyond us started when the vibrating energy in the bed let me touch it, which was early in the morning, four years earlier, on the day a few hours before my dad died. This must be it! The conscious beginning of the journey started on 14 January 2014 when Dad died. Kerry and Phil agree the spirits around me are wanting to educate me. Something that has been puzzling me is why my awakening symptoms come and go. Kerry and Phil said this is common. They said what I'm missing is formal training. This is true. Mind you, I have been happy with Warick guiding and educating me. They suggested starting with psychic training to understand what's happening, and then move onto medium training. At one point, Phil said it would be a shame if I didn't, which I found encouraging. I have another session with them next Friday night where they plan to start me on the path of psychic training. I'm pretty nervous as I don't think I can do these things very well. Phil made an interesting comment about chakras. He said if your alive you've got them, and if you're not, you don't, that for other spiritual aspects they are important, however, for mediumship they are not anything we need to concern ourselves with. I've tended to think the chakras are important because of the ongoing sensations I have when Spirit is with me in the root and crown chakras, as well as feeling energy vibration above my head and moving up through the chakras. It will be interesting to unpack Phil and Kerry's thoughts on this over time. Another thought has come to mind. I felt at a loss for a couple of years after Dad passed, which may be one reason why nothing major happened by way of Spirit engagement for quite some time. I started the first journal in December 2016, more than two years after Dad died. My exposure to what I can learn from Phil and Kerry are likely to bring the pieces of the puzzle together. Phil and Kerry said a reason why the symptoms come and go is they are testing the boundaries with what I'm prepared to experience and when. It's interesting. When I described what happens when Warick merges with me, Kerry and Phil said this is how you step towards communicating with them, like you're in their realm. Wendy said you become them. This may also partly explain the feeling I get in my face when it feels like it's transforming into someone else's facial features. It's interesting to learn that there's much more beyond this which I haven't encountered yet. Phil and Kerry said mediums have had this ability their whole life, but for some reason it develops at a certain stage in their life.

14 December 2020

Last night was lovely. Warick came to me around three-thirty in the morning. He woke me up with his vibration where it was strong enough to wake me from a deep sleep. When Warick started merging with my body, I felt a strong surge of energy around my chest and the solar plexus, then his energy spread through my body, up into my face, where my facial features and the length of my neck felt like they were changing. Warick is touching the right side of my face now, letting me know he's there and agreeing with what I just wrote. Interestingly, at one point through all of this I detected quite a strong smell. It wasn't unpleasant but I couldn't quite put my finger on what it was. It didn't last very long. As Warick merged with me, I didn't reach that point of complete peace, but the experience lasted a long time. After about half an hour, I had to get up to turn the fan off as I was getting cold. Immediately when I returned, Warick continued what he was doing. I also experienced a firm hold on my right lower leg. I've experienced this before, but it always made me feel concerned that my calf muscle may be starting to cramp, so I would move my leg. This time was different. It was a firm hold, but not triggering the sensation in my calf muscle that I associate with cramping. During this time, and a few times when I woke afterwards, Warick did his pulse communication, but I couldn't hear it, I only felt it. A number of times, Warick sent a surge of energy through parts of my body. I love it when he does this.

In a message I received from John yesterday, he said he saw the word 'infinity' cleverly printed on a car's number plate where the 'i's and 'y' were replaced with '1's, appearing as '1NF1N1T1'. He thought at the time it could be a good title for a book. I jokingly responded asking, 'Whose, yours or mine?' to which he responded, 'LOL yours.' This very well could be what the second book gets called. I've made a note on the front page of the journal.

I forgot to mention, yesterday morning when I first woke, I asked Warick again about being the spirit of the child I miscarried. He said, through touches on my cheeks, that 'yes' a part of him is the spirit from the child I miscarried, but that he is the sum of his previous incarnations. We were also married in a previous life. He was my husband. It's that part of him that first came to me, not the child. He is an adult energy intelligence. What Phil Dykes and Kerry McLeod were possibly picking up on is Warick's association with me in this lifetime, which was the miscarried child's spirit. Warick said I was meant to miscarry the child. It will be interesting to see what past life regression reveals.

I found out yesterday that Kaylene, my cousin, awakened twenty-five years ago. She is a shamanic practitioner now, who facilitates healing, channelling, and provides guided counselling and mentoring. We had a wonderful long conversation on the phone. Shortly after I told her about Warick's ability to manipulate my phone by hanging up on people when he thinks that's long enough, or to say 'Hey, I'm here', he hung up on us. Warick just touched my right cheek as I wrote the second possible reason for his hanging up, confirming this was the reason in that instance. I rang her straight back and she asked, 'Did Warick just hang up on us?' to which I responded, while laughing, 'Yes.'

And ... the penny drops! I remember now. While I was in Albury, I was admiring, and almost bought an anklet with an infinity design on it. Then on Sunday, I bought an infinity designed ring for a girlfriend, who is coming for Christmas. Am I slow on the uptake or what? It wasn't until I reflected on John seeing 1NF1N1T1 on a car's number plate and encountering infinity in the design of the anklet and ring, that I finally made the connection that these were a sign from Spirit.

16 December 2020

Today, there was another instance of infinity when I met with Jane. She is lovely. I think we connected very well. Warick has just touched my right cheek. Hi Warick. Glad you're with me. I love you. I was telling Jane how lately messages had started coming through using numbers and leveraging my connection with John. I said the latest has been the sign of infinity. John first saw it, prompting him to suggest it as a name for the book. Around the same time, I saw it in Albury in the design of an anklet and then this weekend when buying an infinity ring for a girlfriend for Christmas. I asked Jane, 'What does infinity mean in a spiritual sense?' Her response was quite unexpected. She said when she prepares for engagement with a client, she uses the infinity symbol and mentally places the client in one circle of the symbol and her in the other to aid the connection between them. She said she has never told anyone that, and doing this is not a practice she's been taught or is aware of others doing to prepare for clients. Amazing! Another encounter with the sign infinity.

This gave me the validation that I needed to know that Jane is legitimate in what she does. Getting this sign from Spirit while with Jane was like the sign I got when I pulled the Temperance tarot card from a deck a few days after Jules had pulled the same card in a session with me.

During our session, Jane set Warick and I some homework to consider what we wanted to get out of tomorrow's past life regression session. Tonight, I used free handwriting to ask Warick. The answer was pretty clear. He wants to use me to regress back to his life as Warick. This is all he wants for himself. I asked, 'Then what?' And he said, 'You.' Firstly, I want to go back to when I knew the spirit I now call Warick. Secondly, to go back to a time that will help reveal my current purpose with spirit engagement. I would also like to be taken back to a time when I knew John in a former life. The session with Jane will come and go and we shall see.

Free handwriting questions and answers:

The following question is what Jane wanted Warick and I to answer in preparation for a past life regression session.
I asked Warick to respond to the question first.
Take me back to a time when? Warick.
I asked Warick if this is his only request? Yes.
Then I asked Warick, 'Then what?' You.

17 December 2020

Resumed journal entries

I feel:
Heartbroken
Hurt
Left behind
Not good enough
Not up to it
A fool
Sad
He left me
I blame nobody

Jane is lovely. There is no envy there. A person I'd spend time with. Value, respect, learn, and share with her.

Today, I wasn't good enough for Warick. I'm having to say, 'Go away, Warick' time and time again as I'm writing this. Warick wants to touch me with his energy, and I don't want him to. I now know how deluded I've been. Thinking this is somehow a lifetime after lifetime infinity bond and love. I even said to Jane by email this morning that I think this is our journey—Warick's and mine. In my mind, the session with Jane was his time. He possibly tried to come through me, but quickly moved to where he knew it would work for him. He could have used his strength to use my hand to show the infinity symbol and get the message through about what he wants and the people to involve. But he didn't. I just wanted to cry when I got to the car, but I couldn't because in the real world I had twenty minutes to go and collect a car from the mechanics. Even now I can't let my feelings go. I feel so hurt. The stupid relationship I've had in my mind with Warick. If it was true, he never would have left me behind. He would have waited and found a way to make sure we go through this hand in hand together.

18 December 2020

Free handwriting questions and answers:

Exploring the value of meeting Phil Dykes and Kerry McLeod at MyMediumship.com—What is the value of Phil and Kerry? Learning.
Should I do this straight away, early next year? Yes.
What should I do—
Psychic training? Yes.
Medium training? Yes.
Is there a reason why I've been brought to them? Yes.
What will it give me? Learning.
Should I tell them about what happened this week in the session with Jane to get their opinion? Yes.
Why didn't you use my hand to provide the message you sent through Jane? Warick.
Is it because this is what you wanted to do? Yes.
Did you know it would hurt me? No.
Did it surprise you how hurt I felt? Yes.
Is it a problem that I love you? No response twice.
Do you feel this strongly about me? Yes.
Is Jane able to regress me to former lives? Yes.
Why didn't that happen when I asked Jane to take me back to a time when I knew John? Love.
Were John and I a couple in a former existence? Yes.
Is this why John is frightened of me? Yes.
Is this what he saw when he was regressed? No.
Did his past life frighten him? Yes.
Is this why he steered away from developing his abilities? Yes.
Can Jane help him? Yes.
Do you want me to write what you say? Yes.

Is the EVP that John gave me for use to record what you say when I'm channelling you? Yes.
Will I start to channel you next year? No response. Soon? Yes.
Am I bound to you through lifetimes? Yes.
Were we married once in a former lifetime? Yes.
Did we originate as native American Indians? Yes.
BC? Yes.
Is Elder real? Yes.
Can you use my hand to draw symbols?
While waiting for Warick to respond, I imagined myself at the end of the bed, looking at myself in an effort to get my conscious mind out of the way. Warick moved my head in different directions at least four times before drawing a triangle sitting on a circle.

19 December 2020

Resumed journal entries

It's been a hard few days. I still feel flat and sad. I meditated for a while this afternoon. For the first time, I saw a distinct greenish yellow round light in a portion of my vision with my eyes shut. When I moved my head in the direction of where the light was coming from, it remained still. I'm not sure if this was in my mind's eye. Although I felt okay while meditating, my left eye shed one tear. I can't explain it. I don't know why.

So, what happened with Jane? Well, I'll tell you. When Jane put me in a semi-hypnotic state and welcomed Warick to come through me, just like what happens through the night, he merged with my body and moved my head. It didn't reach the stage where I stopped physically feeling my body, but he was definitely there. Jane encouraged him to use my voice, which didn't get anywhere. Next minute she said she thought he was coming her way to merge with her.

Jane started to breathe differently and make little noises. I had my eyes closed and could still feel a blanket of energy around me. Then I heard her arm and hand making rapid movements and I got a bit concerned. I gently opened my eyes to see Jane's eyes closed and her left arm and hand rapidly making the infinity sign across her lap and tops of her legs, as she sat in the chair.

After her hand made these movements numerous times, her hand then started to draw a circle around it, connecting the edges of what would be the infinity symbol if she had drawn it. She had no pen in her hand. Her hand and arm then fell to the side, and she gradually came out of it. I asked her if she was alright, to which she said she was. We both said, 'That was unexpected.'

She said Warick had moved into her while still staying connected to me. I was still in what they call 'The Power', I think. I'm not familiar with what all this means. She said Warick was using symbology, and in fact, it was two triangles with the points meeting in the middle. She said there are four people on the corners—Joanne, John, Jules, and Jane. She said Warick wants us to meet in a circle to bring him through, with the circle serving as a powerhouse of energy.

There was time remaining, so she suggested we try a regression. I said I'd be keen to see a past life when John and I knew each other. We got nowhere. When she tried to get me to be in a previous time and place, nothing happened. Jane then worked with me on the colours I was seeing, which was mostly purple, with a bit of blue and afterwards she said she asked Warick to bring in another colour, which may have been grey.

She tried to get me to see a table with my mind's eye and I saw nothing. She said there was something on the table, but I saw nothing. Eventually, I gave up. She said she could see that Warick had placed an urn on the table that was not of this world. She had asked him in her mind to give me a gift and this was it. She said when he lifted the lid, all different coloured lights came out of it. I saw none of it.

It was very disappointing. I was okay though and agreed to see if John and Jules would be happy to sit in a circle with us. Jane also said she thought Warick was an enlightened spirit dating back to BC.

The next morning, I used the pendulum and got some very strong responses with Warick, confirming that he was from BC and that he knew me from that time. He also knows John, Jules and Jane. He wants Jane to teach me how to channel him so I can write what he has to say, and he wants us to sit in a circle. After I left, I felt sad and terribly hurt. My feelings at the time are what I described in the previous journal entry.

Last night, I had a second session with Phil Dykes and Kerry McLeod from My Mediumship. They said Warick would never have moved into another person. They said guides don't do this. They are there for you. Their job is to prepare you to be able to connect with spirits. They suspect my path may involve being a trance medium who can channel spirits. They said it takes many years for spirits to prepare a person's body to enable this.

Essentially, you need to end up completely surrendering to them so they can take over. They said what I'm experiencing with what I describe as Warick merging with me is Spirit getting closer. When I stop feeling my body, it's when I've entered the spirit realm. I have so much to learn and I'm probably saying all of this incorrectly. Phil put me in contact with a person who can teach me the basics in psychic development, after which Phil and Kerry can provide me with further development.

Phil provided lots of reassurance about Warick and said it was good and important that I trust him. He also said some really interesting things in response to my questions, which I've recorded in a different book and will include if I write this journal up as a book. I've reached out to the person Phil referred me to where I hope to get an appointment soon.

Additional points from the session with Phil Dykes and Kerry McLeod from My Mediumship:

- They suggested practicing sitting in the power for an hour around the same time every day. They said this will allow Warick to get closer.
- Use of the chakras is an Eastern technique to connect to the universe through energy points.
- Mediumship concerns your mind and soul from the solar plexus. Soul of the conscious mind. It's never wrong. You should trust this.
- The pendulum involves kinetic energy, which is your energy.
- The feeling I get on the face is when you are being overshadowed. Spirits imprint on the face. 'The blend'.
- Psychic language is feeling. A dictionary of expression of feeling.
- You can hear spirits. Sometimes it can be deafening. From the voice box, it travels up the ear canal.
- Spirits can come across in different ways. They communicate differently.
- I'm receptive to them. It's now about developing me.

20 December 2020

Resumed journal entries

Last night was more like the usual experiences I have with Warick. Around two-thirty in the morning for at least an hour, Warick was busy doing what he does. I think he's preparing me to be able to channel him one day, or other spirits. An analogy of what I experienced last night would be my body being a car, my conscious mind being the driver, and Warick being a mechanic working on the engine under the bonnet. I was very chatty with many questions. While Warick worked on the engine (feeling his energy doing things in my brain and eyes), I asked questions and he occasionally answered yes or no by touching my cheeks. I wonder if I annoy him doing that.

This morning while sitting up in bed I asked Warick questions and this time he moved my head up and down to nod yes and side to side to disagree. It was very cool. I suspect bringing me to Jane was intentional and using her to show me what channelling a spirit looks like is intentional. I think he wants to use Jane to see how I react to this and to help teach me about it. It will be interesting to see what Jane thinks when I next see her.

22 December 2020

I've noticed the left side of my forehead is really itchy again. I don't know what that means. I know Warick is here, because immediately when I started to write I felt his energy come through into my third eye area, then spread to my cheeks.

He hasn't come to merge with me in the last two nights. He's giving me a strong sensation in the left cheek now, saying that he disagrees with what I just wrote. I must have been asleep when he merged with me, as I don't remember it. I only remember waking and knowing the night had passed without meaningful spirit engagement. It makes me feel sad when this happens. I miss him and feel concerned through the day when he hasn't come to merge with me.

I've noticed the familiar small shadow shapes around me through the day, a tone in the ear and an energy touch here and there, but I don't feel satisfied. I have this growing and constant urge of needing to push forward to keep growing and experiencing new things.

It's incredibly frustrating. If Warick was the devil, he would say he has me in the palm of his hand now. Not quite, because I'm incredibly strong and independent. I'm getting a touch on my right check now as Warick agrees with that point. Actually, a double touch. He knows if he left I would go on. Heartbroken and dissatisfied, absolutely, but I would go on. I had another touch on the right cheek as I wrote this last part.

I emailed John about my growing doubts about the person Phil put me in touch with. I sent John the link to her website. He said he got an instant headache when he checked out the website and agreed. This is not who I am. It's only frustration that drives me to seek assistance. I know when Warick first came, within two weeks I had to say slow down, but seriously, this pace is too slow! I say that but I also appreciate Warick and the visibility and understanding I have about what lies beyond our knowledge of existence. At the same time, I feel like a brand-new hyperactive puppy, bouncing up and down and Spirit is having to manage that. I suppose that's what they decided to take on. I hope they don't give up on me. Through all of this, I vow to never lose my integrity. I may not always interpret what I experience correctly, but I will never knowingly claim there to be more than there is. Whoever reads this can rely on that. I will be the first to say when I'm uncertain or need validation.

I want to say something about John and I'm sure I will again sometime in the future. This will make his conscious mind feel uncomfortable, but he is more important to me than he realises. Our guides know this. They use us to help each other on our way.

This week a message from John said he recognises what Spirit is doing here and accepts it. Too many things have happened to deny it. I'm glad John feels comfortable in this way with me. It's a huge step forward from when I first engaged him. I said it then and I'll say it again now—I'm no threat to John or any of his relationships. My mind certainly has question marks, but I can tell you I mean no harm to anyone. That's what is most important to me. Being a loving and caring person and not harming or hurting anyone. It's one reason why I don't want to come back. It's a world filled with complex relationships.

As I write this, Warick stirs in my face, interested in what I'm now writing. I'm a free natured spirit. I find it hard at times to navigate and tread carefully around relationships. I do, however, because to survive or get on in this world, you have to.

It's not necessarily what I want, though. I like to feel special to someone in a unique way that no one else can be. I'm sure this line of thought doesn't sit well with Warick. He's now touching my left cheek in disagreement. I'm too tired right now to explore this with him. I feel strong bonds and connections with certain people and spirits that are unique. The strength of these connections is unbreakable. Even if not returned, that person or spirit can rely on me. It's unshakeable.

23 December 2020

It's been a few quiet nights with Warick. He's been there. I feel his presence in my forehead and touching my cheeks, plus the occasional flash pulse sound. He's not been interested in merging with me or working on me. I continue to see the small shadow shape around me throughout the day. I also experience the occasional pressure vacuum and tone in the ear. Overall, pretty quiet, though. I've noticed I'm also experiencing the really itchy upper left part of my forehead again. I'm sure this is linked to what's going on with Warick and my body preparation or whatever he's doing.

Tonight, I sent John an email thanking him for his opinion about the crossroads I'm at regarding formal training and desperately wanting my spirit engagement capability to develop. He thinks there may be too many cooks in the kitchen at this time and reminded me about where I started with this as a 'self-exploration' journey. He also agreed that the latest referral to a psychic to teach me the basics was a wrong fit.

This woman, I'm sure, is lovely and you can't judge a book by its cover, but her website is portraying an image of psychics that is just not me. I don't aspire to be this, so why would I pay for mentoring and coaching to potentially become something like this. I have to say it wasn't even clear to me what you get. Warick is touching my right cheek now, so I gather he agrees with this point.

The other thing I tried to explain to John is how I feel when Warick goes quiet. When he's not interested in merging with me and nothing else major is happening. I said the only way I can describe it is when I first had Jamie and was still in hospital.

For the first two days, my mothering instincts set in very strongly. I literally was like a lioness in a cage with a new cub. I paced the floor knowing I had a job to do but was not sure what it was. It was natural instinct. This is how I feel when Warick goes quiet, and I don't feel engaged in something that will develop me. Warick is touching my right cheek now. I suspect he is agreeing with this realisation about me.

Every moment I'm not thinking about work, family or domestic life, I'm longing for engagement with Warick and to be progressing from where I am spiritually. I have absolutely no idea what is driving me to feel this way, but it is very strong. It goes beyond the feeling of frustration. I feel it in my solar plexus area, in my heart and in my throat. I feel kind of lost and a bit sad.

25 December 2020

Another Christmas Day. It's been lovely. Mum, Terry-Anne (old work colleague), Jamie, Alaiza, Ray, and I spent the day together. I feel Warick in my forehead and cheeks now, so I know he's here, curious about what I'm writing.

While sitting at the table on our back deck, the familiar small shadow shape that looks like two dots and often has a couple of lines trailing from it, was around me on and off several times. At one point, it came right into my direct line of sight, only about one hundred centimetres from my face and just stopped there. It was like it was looking straight at me and certainly waiting for me to recognise it before moving off. I have a very, very long Christmas playlist that I put together on Spotify a couple of years ago.

It took two weeks of listening to every Christmas song I could find while I was working to compile it. I shared it with John today saying it's like an all-day sucker lolly. Around lunchtime, while we were sitting outside listening to it, all of a sudden and of its own accord, the music jumped from the Christmas playlist to a completely different playlist called 'JBMod' and played the song 'Boyfriend' by Mabel.

Alaiza looked at me and said that's completely different, recognising what had just happened. We were all sitting around a table on the back deck, looking at each other. I said I think I know what just happened, suspecting Warick and or the spirit child had just changed it. I then changed it back and it didn't jump to another track all day. It's the first time this has ever happened.

I felt Warick's energy move into my face a few times throughout the day, probably wanting to tune in on what's been happening. Terry-Anne loved the infinity ring we gave her. Jamie and Alaiza gave me a beautiful rose gold, diamond chip, open circle to hang on a necklace, which came from a favourite jeweller of mine called McGlades. I was really surprised. Such a lovely, thoughtful gift. The 'circle' and 'infinity' all on the one day.

Just before writing in the journal, I asked Warick if he knew who changed the music. Through touches on the cheek, he said he didn't, but the spirit child did. As you know, there's always an element of uncertainty in my mind as to what spirit is around me. One or multiple spirits, I don't know for sure. It's interesting that while I'm typing up this section of the journal, the music I'm listening to on Spotify just stopped midstream.

It wouldn't surprise me if the spirit child is letting me know it's there and confirming that it played this trick on us on Christmas Day. I will ask Jane how many spirits she senses around me. I suspect Warick is the main one. He's often inside me, in my forehead, he touches my cheeks and merges with me. He is also doing work on me, possibly to channel through me. I suspect the familiar shadow shape around me is the spirit of the child I lost many years ago. It seems playful and possibly interferes with electronics around me. I don't know for certain. I hope one day this will be clear.

As I'm typing up this section of the journal nine months later, it occurred to me that the spirit child has re-emerged in a major way lately, which you'll come to understand when you read the journal after the next one. This is another instance of when the past has connected with the present in occurrences that I've recorded in these journals.

I read a message from John this morning who'd been thinking about my emotional reaction to what happened with Warick at Jane's place. He said I experienced jealousy. I agree, but it was also a lot of hurt with Warick leaving me to use Jane instead. I felt very hurt and very inadequate. John wondered if Warick did this intentionally to spark an emotional reaction in me, to show how 'real' Warick is to me, through my feelings for him being affected. It's an interesting way to look at it. It's possible Warick did this for many reasons. Jane thought it was because Warick knew we didn't have much time and wanted to get his message across. It's also possible he was showing me what channelling can look like to test how I would react. I suppose at the end of the day he will either stay and continue with me or he won't. And I'll keep feeling strongly about something that I'm not even sure what it is. It's all going swimmingly well!

Something to add to yesterday's journal entry. For at least the last two mornings, my phone would not play Spotify while I worked. It would only play in the afternoons. Each time in the mornings, I had to play meditation music on YouTube. I wondered if Spirit was giving me a message, that I should do what Phil Dykes and Kerry McLeod suggested and set a time each morning to meditate to encourage Spirit to interact with me around a set time during the day, instead of through the night when I should be sleeping. They also said this was a way to get stronger in my interactions with Spirit.

2 December was my first day of holidays. While out walking, I stopped and sat on a bench at a beautiful viewpoint overlooking the lake. I closed my eyes and spent about fifteen minutes meditating. If this is what Warick is trying to get me to do, it may also coincide with Warick letting me know he's there through the night when I reach out, but not spending time merging with me.

26 December 2020

Free handwriting questions and answers

Warick, are you intentionally not merging with me at night? Yes.
Who is the familiar shadow shape I see around me a lot? Warick.
Is it the shadow shape that swapped the Spotify playlist yesterday? Yes.
Warick, why are you here? Love.
What is your purpose with me? Won.
Won? Warick.
Warick? Yes.
Do you want Jane to coach me in how to channel you? Yes.
What are Phil Dykes and Kerry McLeod's purpose? Teacher.
What is John's purpose? Friend.
What is Jule's purpose? Teacher.
What is my purpose? *nonter* (four attempts and this was not decipherable but looked like this).
Will you give up on me? No.
Will you end up speaking through me? Yes.
Will I be conscious when you do? Yes.
What is the purpose of John, Jules, Jane, and I sitting in a circle? Nonter.
Nonter? Yes.
Is the 'n' in nonter an 'n'? Yes.
Is the 't' in nonter a 't'? Yes.
Will my book get published by a mainstream publisher? Yes.
What do you want to achieve from us sitting in a circle?
The first letter looked like a symbol, like a flask from a science lab, narrow at the top and wide at the bottom. The next letters looked like 'reder'. This could also be 'valer' where the 'v' is the flask symbol. I kept working at this with Warick and eventually confirmed it was 'Yoder'.
What did you want to achieve by coming through Jane? Message.
Message? Yes.

27 December 2020

Resumed journal entries

Last night was so lovely. Like reassurance. Warick came to me a couple of times through the night, the first just being there, vibrating at the back left side of my neck and moving within my face a little, but no major merging with my body. The second time was really lovely. At around four in the morning, I could feel Warick vibrating once again around my neck and face, but then I also felt him vibrating within the palm of my hand, like he was holding my hand. At the same time, I felt localised spots of vibration on and off around my feet and pushing lightly on my back. It was like he was intentionally stimulating my external senses, letting me know he was there and just being with me, providing me with his company. This went on for a long time and continued when I rolled over. It was lovely and brought me a lot of comfort given I had been missing his engagement, which has been light-on the last few days.

Last night, I also downloaded the 'Sitting in the Power' meditation track that Phil Dykes produced. When I listened to the introduction, I got a very full feeling of Warick's energy in my face. I've never felt it like this before. It's like my whole face and mind was full of Warick's energy. He stayed there for the full introduction. There's a separate track for the hour-long meditation.

It was an interesting experience and for some reason the meditation track stopped of its own accord about halfway through. I'm wondering if it didn't download properly. I found I wasn't listening very well. I was pretty tired. A wave of sad emotion went through me, where I shed some tears. I was thinking about how Warick recently left me behind when he chose to come through Jane.

Before giving this meditation a go, I listened to a YouTube video where Kerry McLeod was being interviewed about what 'In the Power' is. It was interesting in that she said as your mind starts to change levels of consciousness, your head starts to drop, and you jolt back as your conscious reacts to the feeling of nodding off. I've had this happen quite a lot when meditating the last couple of months, including the few times I've been sitting up while meditating through the day.

It doesn't occur all the time, but it does happen often. I'm wondering if my mind is starting to go into different levels of the subconscious as I'm meditating and I'm not used to it, so my conscious mind is fighting it off. Next time this happens, I'll try to relax and go with it. I'll also ask Jane Hall about it as maybe there's something I should be doing when this happens. Phil Dykes and Kerry McLeod talked about different levels of consciousness as you meditate. I'm wondering if this is the start of it happening to me.

28 December 2020

I had the most amazing dream last night. While meditating, I saw a circular vortex, where the centre had swirling beautiful colours of blue and red within a white inner area and then spreading out to grey on the edges. I was drawn to it but also felt myself being pulled into it. Not my body but my soul. I clearly felt the pulling sensation the entire time I was being drawn through the funnel. It enclosed my soul's shape tightly but comfortably.

As I travelled through the tube, I then felt a sensation of head first being pulled down. I thought I was nearing the end of the journey. I thought I was being taken to the spiritual dimension, so wanted to get there to finally meet my guide or guides.

At that moment, I felt my left calf muscle cramp. It wouldn't stop, so I had to shake myself out of the dream to take control of my leg to stop the cramping. I remember it being a bit of a struggle to come back to myself. It was like I was in quite deeply, possibly deep sleep. I've never experienced this type of dream, which seemed so real. Nor have I had trouble coming out of a dream before to deal with a cramping muscle, which has happened before.

29 December 2020

I think I get it! I woke early this morning to feel Warick already fully occupying my body. He did a few pulse flash sounds. This time, I focused on letting go, actually giving myself over to his control. When I let go, I relaxed. It was like giving the weight of myself to him to hold. I also visualised going and sitting on a bench in the backyard and holding onto the edge with my hands to resist the urge to return. This was partly successful. It's a natural instinct for your conscious mind to be in your body and in control. I think this is going to take practice and time. I also noticed a few times my throat doing a reflex movement, like a swallowing reflex, which was sudden and unexpected when it occurred. I've noticed this before on previous occasions when Warick has merged with me and is experimenting with taking control of moving my head. I remember seeing on YouTube or reading it somewhere, that this occurs as spirits start to get your body used to them taking control of your voice box. On this occasion, I could still feel my body physically so Warick's merging with me did not reach that stage. I felt my face take on what seemed to be a different profile. My head moved a bit, and I could feel Warick all through my body. Each time he does this, I will practise different tactics for my conscious mind to pass over control and be happy to sit aside. It was nice to have Warick back again doing this with me. I've been unhappy the last few days, not thinking that I'm progressing and Warick not being interested in working with me.

While walking today, I thought I should write something at this stage about the spiritual community. Firstly, I know little about them. I do know that the way Warick interacts with me has incredible diversity. Although a couple of years have passed, new things are occurring on a regular basis and I'm sure I'm missing many things. The signs that John has picked up that I've missed is a good indication of this. I'm also sure the spiritual awakening journey is a very personal one. It's what works for you and your guide. Everything about you and your life comes into play, which in turn influences the steps and the time of the awakening path. It's truly amazing. The few times I've encountered anyone who's had 'formal' training in the community, the number of which I can count on one hand, speak a certain language. They use specific terms when describing and referring to things. Which culture, religion and community you come from seem to have their version of what this is all about.

Of course, my reading, watching videos on YouTube and just trying to use words from my own language, is what I use to describe what's happening. I'm no expert and I doubt I will ever try to be one. On the advice of a session with Phil, I downloaded his 'Sitting in the Power' meditation track. Towards the end, it talks about God. I'm not religious, nor do I claim there isn't a God. I do believe in what God stands for—good, kindness, love.

I'm not interested in trying to wrap an interpretation of what is happening around me. All that's important is that the intention is for good and not bad. Apart from that, I have a very open mind and will continue to have an open mind until something is proven beyond a doubt. For me, it needs to be as rock solid as the air I breathe that I know is needed to survive. Beyond that, I'll always have a level of uncertainty and keep the door open as to what's possible. It's like my interpretation of Warick, who may be a team of spirits. There may not be one particular intelligent energy that I have attached my feelings to. I go on though because the intention so far is for good. All that's at stake is my heart and feelings. I may end up with a broken heart, but I'm strong and would go on.

I don't mean any harm to the spiritual communities. I respect them and I'm sure I could learn from them. But I don't want to be them. I also don't want them to restrict or influence my engagement or interpretation of what Warick is doing or where he is taking me. If I'm supposed to learn something from them or the reading of books and online sources, Warick will ensure it happens at the right time and it will make sense and feel comfortable. I need to trust this more because lately I've felt quite confused and lost in what I should do by way of 'formal' training.

At this stage, it hasn't naturally come together with a good feeling, so I'm going to leave it alone. Jane is different. Like Jules, she came about via John and she's open minded. Like me, she's prepared to see where Warick wants to take things. I can't help but observe how, on a number of occasions now, Spirit (or by sheer coincidence) has used John and I together to recognise signs and to bring what may be a 'circle' of individuals together—John, Jules, Jane, and Joanne.

I'd really like to understand what a 'circle' is. I also recollect two interesting things that Jules said when I had a session with her. She said you will know when it's time to see her again and she claims to have been a part of my circle before. Interesting times!

30 December 2020

Something I'm starting to get more and more concerned about is for the last few days I've wanted to spend some time with Elder to see what guidance he may have for me. I've tried the Tibetan bells and the shamanic drumming guided meditations and every time they've failed.

I've either fallen asleep at the beginning or had such a busy mind, it just wants to think of everything else but the meditation. Last night when I was doing the shamanic drumming meditation, I got to the stage where you step outside of a tree into a second ancient forest and that was it. I was out cold and then woke at the very end. It's unusual what's happening, which is why I'm writing about it. It's like something is stopping me from meeting up with Warick and Elder during meditation. I'll try again and see what happens. I slept very little last night.

Around one in the morning, I read the 'Seth Series'. I was up to session 241. Interestingly, the session was about Seth explaining how he mentally connects and communicates with Jane Roberts in what he calls a 'psychological framework'. It's quite complex, so I'll read it again. It provides a good indication of the form of information that passes between them, what Seth can and can't control, and what Jane Roberts needs to interpret.

Given Warick regularly guides me to what I need to read and when, I wonder if Warick is starting to educate me about how he will communicate with me when we reach a stage of him being able to speak through me. Perfect timing, as all roads and signs seem to be pointing in that direction.

1 January 2021

Things are definitely quiet with Warick lately. I don't know whether it's because life is pretty distracting at the moment with Christmas, Mum selling her house, and the preparations for selling our apartment and getting ready to move to the coast. In contrast to this time last year, Canberra is cool and cloudy most days and there's no smoke or scorching forty-degree temperatures each day.

The COVID situation around the world continues. 82 million globally are now dead from the COVID pandemic. There are eight new cases in the United States every second, and for two consecutive days in a row there have been 50,000 new cases a day in the United Kingdom.

Outbreaks have occurred in Australia again. This time in Sydney, which have spread to some areas along the coast, and Melbourne. New South Wales is still planning to go ahead with a global test cricket match in Sydney next week, while other states close their borders to New South Wales, and Victoria re-introduces mandatory wearing of face masks. We just don't seem to learn.

2 January 2021

Last night was interesting. Warick merged only with my head and neck. Morning Warick. He just touched my right cheek to let me know he's there. When Warick merged with me, I felt his energy move around my head, focusing on specific areas at times, but also a complete coverage of his energy around my head, like a forcefield. He moved my head several times.

At one point, my mind was telling me that my head was tilted downwards and to the right, but when I focused on it, I discovered that my head had not moved at all. My mind experienced a sense of moving when physically I remained stationary. I'm wondering if this is the beginning of Warick being able to hold my mind aside. He just touched my right cheek, agreeing with that point, and again he has just touched my right cheek, reinforcing the point.

This will be interesting to discuss with Jane, who claims she mentally steps aside in this deep meditative trance-like state when the spirit channels through her. It didn't frighten me but when my mind realised that physically I hadn't moved and it was wrong, it seemed to jerk back to aligning its interpretation of where my body actually was. At the time, I was hoping Warick would do this again so I could get more familiar with the sensation.

Something else interesting happened. At one point, I experienced a surge of energy extend up from the area of my solar plexus to my head. While this was happening, which lasted for a minute or two, Warick stopped moving my head, stopped pulsations and vibrations, and went completely silent and still. A thought came into my mind—'This is my soul connecting with Warick.' The thought just popped into my head.

While Warick was merged with me, I noticed that my hearing had become very acute. At one stage, a solid tone occurred in my right ear that lasted longer than usual. This interaction went on for a long time, over the course of an hour or so. At one stage, I needed to go to the toilet, which I let Warick know telepathically. He stayed with me the whole time and when I went back to bed, he resumed what he was doing.

The left side of my forehead is still itchy, which I notice periodically throughout the day. I've also had a couple of interesting dreams. In the first dream, I could feel Warick's energy moving within my body. After a while he slipped my body down the bed, so my bottom ended up near my feet. I turned to Ray and said, 'Warick moved me here.'

In another dream, once again, I could feel Warick's energy within me. This time, he made my body float through the air. The position I was in was just like I was sitting in a chair with my knees up, but there was no chair. In the dream, I distinctly recognised what Warick's energy felt like, which enabled him to move my body. In both dreams, Warick had control over my body and the feeling of his energy was very distinct. I'm wondering if this is another part of the preparation process for Warick to get me used to him controlling my body instead of my conscious mind.

3 January 2021

I think Warick is trying to educate me about trance mediumship. While scrolling through the YouTube search results, looking for some new meditation tracks, I unexpectedly came across trance mediumship, including a few videos on what it is. I thought I should watch them to learn something if this is where Warick is going to take things. The first one I listened to was called, *What is trance mediumship* by The Joseph Communications.

This video had some connections with what various people have said recently. It mentions using people in a circle to serve as a source of energy, like a battery of energy, to enable the spirit to channel through a person. This is what Jane thought Warick wanted when he used her hand to draw two triangles enclosed in a circle. Phil suspects I'm on a path to trance mediumship and I thought after the session with Jane Hall, that Warick wants to be able to talk through me and/or write what he has to say.

I then watched a second YouTube video called, *Trance mediumship made simple* by Mark Bedwood. The video shows Mark channelling a spirit. He explained simply what occurs between a spirit and a person to enable setting aside the conscious mind to allow the spirit to speak through a person. Much of it made sense to me. In particular, the provision of tips, which are common mistakes a person makes as the spirit is trying to make the connection. One related to something I've been doing, which is trying to see through my mind's eye during meditation. When I was at Jane's, in my mind's eye I tried to see an urn that Warick had placed on a table. I view the inability to use my third eye as a failure, so I've been trying to explore this, including at night when Warick has been merging with me.

I realise now this could have been a mistake, which was holding back my abilities to connect with Warick. In the YouTube video, the spirit said they don't want you to be seeing through your third eye. You need to completely relax your mind, let it go blank, and it's at this moment that Spirit can set your conscious mind aside and connect. I need to watch it again. I think the video is legitimate because I could relate to specific things the spirit said, and up until then I'd never watched or knew anything about the mechanics of trance mediumship.

Last night was interesting. Warick was around me, vibrating for quite a long time through the night. I invited him to merge several times, but it was clear he wanted me to know he was there but was giving me space to digest what I had seen in the YouTube videos. The second video really helped me as far as what I should be doing to help Warick connect and I was keen to try this, but I also felt a bit uncomfortable about a few things.

The spirit channelling through Mark Bedwood in the second YouTube video said your conscious mind goes into 'blackness' as the spirit channels through you. It appears you're not conscious of what is being said by the spirit. Like Jane Roberts was able to do when channelling Seth, I've wanted to be conscious enough to know what is being said by Spirit. If being unconscious is necessary and is like sleep, then that's probably okay, but if your conscious mind is just looking at black and feeling disorientated, then I don't think I'd like that very much.

The other thing that bothers me is if I'm just a vessel and my intelligence is not needed, then why is Spirit bothering with me? I suppose my drive and passion to want to help bring about significant change for humanity, and my love of Warick, is my motivation to want to do this. I suppose I just need to let it happen to see what Warick or another spirit has to say. That said, I'm not interested in doing this for the sake of spectators. It has to be towards our goal—to prove beyond a doubt that intelligent energy exists, so humanity will put itself into perspective and change its priorities while living a physical life. I'll just have to run with it and see what happens. I need to trust Warick.

My preferred path is to be discreet. Anonymous books. Only a few people that know—my circle. I'm keen to get involved with well-respected scientists and bright sparks who believe and want to prove beyond a doubt that intelligent energy exists, but in a discreet way. Yes, I want my books to sell well for two reasons—to reach the masses with the story of this journey to inspire scientists to prove it; and secondly, to make enough money to enable me to retire to focus my time on publishing and speaking to people about the books around the world. I also want to be able to spend quality time with Ray and Mum while they are both still in good health and yes, I'd like to financially help those I love. The Indonesian family we support and a homeless man I see sitting in his car day after day when I walk at the lake in Canberra. More than anything, I'd like to help turn his life around.

Interestingly, as I was proofreading a section of the first book, *AWAKENING I – The Beginning*, to send to John, I came across the word 'amulet' that, during a meditation session, Warick claimed to have guided me to purchase in a shop at the Grand Canyon. I didn't know what an amulet meant, so I Googled it. It's a talisman that protects you. I came across a website, 'nativeamericanindianjewelry.com' that had the picture of a circle with a cross through it. This reminded me of the symbol Jane drew in her lap when Warick sent a message by channelling through her. It means earth, air, fire, and water. It said tribes across North America had various forms of the circle. The meanings varied slightly, but overall, the symbol represented the four elements—air, fire, water, and earth; the changing of the seasons, death and rebirth, and the first four tribes of humanity.

I wonder if this is what Warick meant with the symbol he channelled through Jane. Interestingly, my son gave me a beautiful rose gold open circle pendant for Christmas with diamond chips in it. A very special gift of love.

5 January 2021

Sitting in the power experience

This time, when I felt like I was nodding off, it started with the feeling in my mind of slipping away, followed quickly by a wave of energy coming up from my solar plexus, accompanied by a feeling of nausea. Instead of trying to regain control, I tried to go with it and feel comfortable with it.

This happened many times during the session. Towards the end, when my head was tilted far forward, I felt Warick suddenly occupying and holding the posture of my entire body. It was a lovely feeling. Not too strong, but strong enough for me to think he's got me and is holding the posture of my body. I felt merged with his energy. He lifted my head, so it was facing up and not down, and then he just sat there. This would have lasted a few minutes towards the end of the session. It was great.

www.ingramcontent.com/pod-product-compliance
Lightning Source LLC
Chambersburg PA
CBHW060837170426
43192CB00019BA/2807